Social Europe
A Continent's Answer to Market Fundamentalism

Edited by Detlev Albers,
Stephen Haseler and
Henning Meyer

Published by the European Research Forum at London Metropolitan University

Under the umbrella of the Party of European Socialists (PES) and in cooperation with the Gramsci Foundation (Rome), the Renner Institute (Vienna) and
the Ovidiu Sincai Institute (Bucharest)

European Research Forum at London Metropolitan University
Department of Law, Governance and International Relations
London Metropolitan University
Old Castle Street
London, E1 7NT
United Kingdom
www.europeanresearchforum.com

First published in 2006

ISBN: 0-9547448-3-7 (paperback)

A catalogue record for this book is available from the British Library

Design and Layout: Ben Eldridge

Printed by Lightning Source

Lightning Source UK Ltd.
6 Precedent Drive
Rooksley
Milton Keynes
MK13 8PR, UK

Lightning Source Inc. (US)
1246 Heil Quaker Blvd.
La Vergne, TN USA 37086

Contents

Notes on the Contributors   v

Preface   ix

Acknowledgements   xi

1. Introduction   1
    Detlev Albers, Stephen Haseler and Henning Meyer

2. From the Constitutionalisation of   9
    Europe to a European Constitution
    Peter Brandt and Dimitris Tsatsos

3. The Future of Europe   33
    Giuliano Amato

4. The Great Adventure of Europe   39
    Detlev Albers

5. The Consequences of 29th May 2005   53
    Elisabeth Guigou

6. How to Overcome the European Crisis?   57
    Massimo D'Alema

7. Danger for Europe   63
    Garrelt Duin and Martin Schwanholz

8. Present and Future of the European Union   73
    Alfred Gusenbauer

9. A Democratic Left Vision for Europe   85
    David Clark, Neil Kinnock, Michael Leahy,
    Ken Livingstone, John Monks and Stephen Twigg

10. **Some Reflections on the European Social Model**   **111**
  Vladimir Špidla

11. **Renewing not Rolling Back Social Europe**   **117**
  Poul Nyrup Rasmussen

12. **The Social Dimension of the European Union**   **125**
  Angelica Schwall-Düren

13. **Reflections on the Meaning of 'Social' and 'Liberal'**   **133**
  Jenny Andersson

14. **Social Europe and European Identity**   **145**
  Donald Sassoon

15. **The Real Underlying Debate in Europe is not the EU**   **161**
  Constitution but, Rather, the Future of Capitalism
  Jeremy Rifkin

16. **What is the Way Forward for the European Economy?**   **167**
  Dominique Strauss-Kahn

17. **What is the Progressive Case for Gender Equality?**   **179**
  Zita Gurmai

18. **Women in Social Democratic Politics**   **187**
  Wendy Stokes

19. **The Freedom We Mean**   **203**
  Hubertus Heil

20. **Putin's Russia: Love and Hatred Towards the EU**   **207**
  Silvo Pons

Notes on the Contributors

Detlev Albers is Professor of Politics at Bremen University. He was also chairman of the SPD Bremen for almost a decade and still serves on the federal executive committee of the SPD and in the party's Basic Values Commission.

Giuliano Amato is the Italian Interior Minister and a former Prime Minister. He also served as Vice-Chairman of the European Convention that elaborated the European Constitutional Treaty.

Jenny Andersson is based at the Department of Economic History at Uppsala University. She is also a Visiting Fellow at the Centre for European Studies at Harvard University.

Peter Brandt is Professor of European and German History at the University of Hagen. He is an expert in comparative constitutional history and taught at the TU Berlin before taking up his current position.

David Clark was Robin Cook's special advisor from 1994 to 2001. He is now a freelance political consultant and commentator, as well as a Senior Research Fellow at the Federal Trust for Education and Research in London.

Massimo D'Alema is the Italian Foreign Secretary and Deputy Prime Minister. He is also President of *Democratici di Sinistra*, the biggest party in Romano Prodi's coalition.

Garrelt Duin is a Member of the German *Bundestag* and the chairman of the SPD in Lower Saxony. He is also a former Member of the European Parliament.

Elisabeth Guigou is a French Member of Parliament. She also occupied several senior minister positions, including the portfolios of European and social affairs.

Zita Gurmai is a Hungarian Member of the European Parliament and President of PES Women, which brings together women politicians and activists from European socialist, social democratic and labour parties.

Alfred Gusenbauer is the leader of the Austrian Social Democratic Party SPÖ. He is Vice-President of the Socialist International and holds a PhD in politics.

Stephen Haseler is Professor of Government at London Metropolitan University. In the 1970s he served as Deputy Mayor of London. He is the author of numerous books on social democracy, British politics and international relations.

Hubertus Heil is the General Secretary of the SPD and a Member of Parliament for a constituency in Lower Saxony.

Neil Kinnock is Head of the British Council and Baron of Bedwellty in the County of Gwent. He is a former leader of the British Labour Party and Vice-President of the European Commission.

Michael Leahy is General Secretary of the British trade union Community. He is also Chairman of the National Trades Union Steel Co-ordinating Committee.

Ken Livingstone became Mayor of London in May 2000 and was re-elected in 2004. He was elected as a Labour MP for Brent East in 1987 and held the seat until 2001.

Henning Meyer is the Associate Director of the European Research Forum at London Metropolitan University and Managing Editor of 'Social Europe: the journal of the european left'.

John Monks is General-Secretary of the European Trade Union Confederation and Visiting Professor to the School of Management at UMIST, Manchester.

Poul Nyrup Rasmussen is a former Prime Minister of Denmark. He is a Member of the European Parliament and President of the Party of European Socialists.

Silvio Pons is Director of the Gramsci Foundation and Professor of East European History at Rome University.

Jeremy Rifkin is the President of the Foundation on Economic Trends in Washington DC, and the author of *The European Dream: How Europe's Vision of the Future is Quietly Eclipsing the American Dream*.

Donald Sassoon is Professor of Comparative European History at Queen Mary's, University of London and author of the landmark work *One Hundred Years of Socialism*.

Angelica Schwall-Düren is a German Member of Parliament and Vice Chairwoman of the SPD in the *Bundestag*.

Martin Schwanholz is a Member of the German *Bundestag* and sits on the Committee for European Union affairs.

Vladimir Špidla is a former Prime Minister of the Czech Republic and currently European Commissioner for employment, social affairs and equal opportunities.

Wendy Stokes is a Senior Lecturer at London Metropolitan University and an expert in women's politics.

Dominique Strauss-Kahn is a French Member of Parliament and a former Economic and Finance Minister. He is also Professor of Economics at Sciences Po in Paris.

Dimitris Tsatsos is Professor Emeritus of the Universities of Hagen and Panteion, Athens, and a board member of the Institute for European Constitutional Sciences, Hagen. He is also Associate Professor at the Law School of the University of Düsseldorf.

Stephen Twigg is Director of the Foreign Policy Centre. He was a British Member of Parliament between 1997 and 2005 and was Parliamentary Secretary to the Leader of the House of Commons and a junior minister in the Department for Education and Skills.

Preface

This book consists of the core contributions to the first volume of 'Social Europe: the journal of the european left' and some new parts exclusively published in this edition. It brings together a range of topical debates that were initiated over the last year and that need to be pursued in even more depth in the months and years to come. Despite the frequent use of the catchphrase 'Social Europe' in contemporary political discourse, there is surprisingly little comprehensive up-to-date literature that addresses the crucial questions surrounding this issue. Therefore, this edited volume is intended to provide a point of reference and orientation for a key debate. It also seeks, hopefully, to clarify and inspire.

Since May 2005 we have published four journal issues dealing with different dimensions of the 'Social Europe' debate that stimulated and involved thousands of readers not just in Europe but across the world. In these times when political involvement is on the retreat in many societies, it is even more important to reach out to people and provide easily accessible information that helps to structure the debate about the scope and direction of politics in contemporary affairs.

The discussion of 'Social Europe' is an ongoing process and in these essays the authors have only just started to ponder the political implications and necessary innovations inherent in the idea. And we would like to invite all of you to participate in the shaping of arguably one of the most important political issues for Europe's future. Visit our website www.social-europe.com for the latest 'Social Europe' journal issues – published on a quarterly basis – and further information about up-to-date research and events. You can also contact us at info@social-europe.com if you have suggestions or want to raise a particular matter.

In this book, we have managed to bring together some of the biggest names in politics and academia providing what we think is a solid foundation for the development of the 'Social Europe' debate. We hope you find the following pages interesting reading.

Detlev Albers, Stephen Haseler and Henning Meyer
London, June 2006

Acknowledgements

We would like to thank the editorial board and friends of 'Social Europe: the journal of the european left' for their help and support. Also there are numerous individuals who provided crucial help, advice and inspiration. They are Chloé Aublin, Stephen Barber, Michael Braun, Ruth Davis, Patrick Diamond, Chris Dixon, Timo Ehl, Ben Eldridge, Ditte Frederiksen, Erich Fröschl, Ian Gardiner, Katerina Hadjimatheou, Andreas Helle, Anne Juganaru, Herwig Kaiser, Jeannette Ladzik, Veronique Levieux, Gero Maass, Klaus Mehrens, Marco Ricceri, David Schoibl, Adrian Severin, Giuseppe Vacca, Sam Whimster and Jon Worth. We are grateful to all of them. Last but not least we would like to express our gratitude to our authors and readers.

Social Europe: An Introduction

By Detlev Albers, Stephen Haseler and Henning Meyer

Competing Models of Capitalism – the Core Questions

After two decades in which social democracy has been on the defensive – and neo-liberal market fundamentalism has seemed triumphant – the left-of-centre is finally reasserting itself. By the summer of 2006 a host of political events in Europe had revealed what may be a sea-change in opinion. Italy has joined Spain in electing a centre-left government; the SPD had done better than many expected in the German elections; in France a socialist win in the coming presidential election has begun to look a distinct possibility; and, even in Britain, for long the home of neo-liberal economics, the return of the Labour government in 2005 may well lead to a new left-of-centre consensus.

What these political changes represent is a real turning-point. European publics, from Germany to Spain, and France to Italy, are clearly saying that there is a limit to their acceptance of 'free market' economics and the erosion of their welfare states.

The obvious desire to maintain a strong 'social dimension' to modern capitalism means that 'Social Europe' is now not just a set of policies but is also coming to define the continent. In a globalised world in which American and Chinese capitalisms are major competitor models, 'Social Europe' is even giving Europe an identity.

'Social Europe' is now also being sustained by better economic prospects. Long derided by neo-liberal critics as 'sclerotic', the European economy is now beginning to recover and grow; and the Euro is at an all-time high and looks set to become even stronger. By comparison, there is little doubt that the erstwhile triumphant US 'Anglo-Saxon' economic model is creaking, even in some respects becoming dysfunctional. And the huge US trade and government deficits (and imbalances), and the massive private debt levels and housing bubbles, are taking the shine off the growth figures.

Also, in the US and British economies globalisation is producing unacceptable inequalities. In these economies not only is the gap between rich and poor growing, but social mobility is coming to an end. A rigid new class system – in which the middle class is eroded, and inheritance is rewarded more than work – is emerging. These growing inequalities are not just morally objectionable, they are socially unsustainable, leading to fractured societies which, unless they are repaired, can breed hopelessness, even violence and extremism.

Above all, neo-liberalism is being revealed as having no answers to the big questions. How do Western societies compete with the low cost base and huge labour reserves of China and India? How do we preserve our welfare states in a globalised economy in which 'competitiveness' is the name of the game? Can a global market system secure cheap and plentiful energy in the short run and lessen dependence on non-renewables in the long run? How can we develop sustainable growth and democracy in the workplace?

Social democrats need to take the lead in fashioning new thinking by getting to grips with these real questions, many of them highly sensitive. We need to look in a fresh way at the traditional economic questions such as taxation and employment. Can we fashion a taxation philosophy that assures that the super-rich pay their fair share and that the over-burdened middle income groups are not penalised? Can we construct a fair and harmonised Europe-wide taxation system that does not allow footloose capital to play one nation off against each other in a 'race to the bottom'? Can we limit the inordinate power of modern corporations without losing their creative power? Above all, can we usher in economic democracy through new corporate structures?

Also, we need some clear, fresh and unafraid thinking about the crucial question of 'free-trade' in our globalised world. 'Free-trade' is a myth, but also a mantra. We need to ask some urgent questions: is the West's commitment to extreme 'free-trade' policies fatally weakening our employment base in Europe? Do both the European Union (EU) and the developing world need to protect their home markets in order to maintain and achieve minimum standards? Social democrats should not be afraid to tackle these controversial questions. Simply to avoid the issue by denouncing every protective measure as 'protectionism' is to close the mind. Indeed, we need to explore how a socially just trading system would work, and if market fundamentalists wish to label this project as 'neo-protectionist' so be it.

What Does the European Social Model Mean?
We also need to define more clearly what the European Social Model (ESM) or 'Social Europe' (these terms are used interchangeably here) actually means. Anthony Giddens says that the European Social Model is 'not a unitary concept, but a mixture of values, accomplishments and aspirations', and the only commonality between them is that they all refer to the welfare state. And Giddens adds: 'In spite of the fact that it is so central, the idea is somewhat elusive when we try to pin it down with any precision'. (Giddens 2006)

Yet Giddens himself tries to do so, and he sets out five criteria as prerequisites:

- A developed and interventionist state, as measured in terms of level of GDP taken up by taxation.
- A robust welfare system, that provides effective social protection, to some considerable degree for all citizens, but especially for those most in need.
- The limitation, or containment, of economic and other forms of inequality.
- A key role in sustaining these institutions is played by the 'social partners', the unions and other agencies promoting workers' rights.
- Each trait has to go along with expanding overall economic prosperity and job creation (Giddens 2006)

The power of Giddens' list of criteria lies in the fact that it deliberately extends the analysis to the socio-economic and political levels, instead of just limiting itself to comparing different social security systems, as happens all too often.

However, we take the view that Giddens' valuable list should be seen as representing a kind of minimum criteria; and that if a country falls seriously short of only one of these requirements it cannot claim to be in line with the European Social Model. Also, there is a strong case that Giddens' criteria are too restrictive for they pay too little attention to the dynamic change potential of the 'principle of democracy'. Neither the 'developed and interventionist state' nor the 'robust welfare system' fell from the sky in any of the European countries. Every step in the construction of the welfare states of Europe was won by fighting the domination of capital with sustained democratic pressure, the product of trade union involvement and social democratic action and policies.

These achievements are now being challenged by the wider global environment. We need to accelerate the catch-up process of new EU and candidate countries with the help of the 'open method of coordination', the EU structural funds and the whole range of tools provided by the *acquis communautaire*, so that the fundamental pillars of the European Social Model can indeed be enforced throughout the Union.

Also, in the Western world the European Social Model cannot only be perceived in a defensive manner, as a protective wall against the negative effects of globalisation. On the contrary, the ESM should be seen as an opportunity and instrument to shape globalisation rather than being shaped by it.

As for the future, it is vital to take the original – national – objectives of the reformist Left, social democrats, socialists and trade unions and reflect further on how to apply them to the new European and global context. At a national level, the primary aim of the Left was to tame capitalism and, by using the tools of democracy, fundamentally transform it into an engine of well-being. This is why the Left defended the social progress involved in the creation of the welfare state and also tried to apply the principle of democracy to the economy.

But in order to secure the future of the European Social Model, we cannot just transpose national concepts and ideas to the European level. It is absolutely essential to accept that national experiences can vary greatly and to figure out how to adjust them to one another in the integration process by thorough-going discussion. In the long run, the European Social Model can only be secured by European integration, for should it falter then global forces will inevitably force down standards.

Also European integration is more, much more, than the economic integration of markets. It has, and needs, a strong political dimension. Indeed, social democrats need to emphasise the primacy of politics; and, within politics, the primacy of democracy. At the same time in future debates about the European Social Model we cannot dilute the universal objectives of economic democracy and social justice, which have been visionary in the past and remain highly relevant today. The ESM needs a much bigger European consciousness with much more conscious European players if it is to be sustained against internal and external pressures. Only if this is achieved will the European Social Model also become attractive to other parts of the world. Who else other than the European Left is fit to lead this undertaking?

Social Europe – The Debate
Against this backdrop, this book seeks to illuminate the discussion about Europe's social dimension with both free academic thinking and 'hands on' policy prescriptions by practitioners. The first part of the book deals with the European Constitution, whose ratification process in 2005 and 2006 revealed deep cracks in Europe's social construction and exposed a widespread perception of the European Union as a driving force of economic injustices rather than a socially sensitive regulator. Peter Brandt and Dimitris Tsatsos begin by embedding the European Constitution in Europe's previous constitutional history as well as analysing European integration in the second half of the 20th century. The new system of governance – the 'hermaphrodite of the new times' as the author calls it – is subsequently analysed by the 'father' of the European Constitutional Treaty and Italian Interior Minister Giuliano Amato. Detlev Albers in his contribution fills the European motto 'united in diversity' with life by identifying the desirable elements of 'diversity' that should also constitute a fundamental part of European 'unity'.

No other political event of the year 2005 heated up the debate about 'Social Europe' as much as the rejection of the European Constitution by the electorates in France and the Netherlands. Is the existing text an adequate basis for developing the social dimension of European integration? Or does it help to further weaken social politics by paving the way for the unrivalled domination of markets in Europe? This issue prominently split the French Left but also revealed frictions elsewhere. In her essay, former French Europe Minister Elisabeth Guigou discusses the consequences of the constitutional debacle and suggests ways back towards a constructive European policy for the Left. In this debate – where now for Europe after the double defeat of the Constitution? – Italian Foreign Secretary Massimo

D'Alema, German Members of Parliament Garrelt Duin and Martin Schwanholz as well as the leader of the Austrian social democrats Alfred Gusenbauer assert their points of view too.

Partly but not solely induced by the political volatility following the Constitution's rejection, the European Left generally requires fresh thinking and a new approach to strengthen the social dimension of European integration. A number of high-profile British authors, including former EU Commission Vice President Neil Kinnock and the Mayor of London Ken Livingstone, tackle this issue by proclaiming a new 'democratic left vision for Europe'. Based on the idea of 'a Europe of values', the authors recalibrate Europe's role in the world and set out their ideas for a socially as well as economically sustainable European Social Model. EU Employment and Social Affairs Commissioner Valdimir Špidla, the President of the Party of European Socialists Poul Nyrup Rasmussen and the senior German Member of Parliament Angelica Schwall-Düren join the deliberations on 'Social Europe' by arguing for a reform but not a simple cutback of social provisions.

The last part of the book represents aspects of the broader discussion about 'Social Europe'. The progressive case for gender equality as well as reflections on terms such as 'freedom', 'social' and 'liberal' are important parts of a general understanding of 'Social Europe'. Also Donald Sassoon's important contribution examining the link between 'Social Europe' and identity provides crucial insights and prescriptions. Several characteristics of this wider debate reflect the tensions between free market domination and a socially moderated form of capitalism mentioned at the beginning of this chapter. Jeremy Rifkin spells out why he sees the debate about the European Constitution as merely a superficial distraction from the real, deep-seated issue about different capitalist models. The whole question about how to bring the European economy back on the path of growth and wealth creation without sacrificing its distinct characteristics is at the heart of former French Finance Minister Dominique Strauss-Kahn's argument. He proposes a more integrated

economic governance in Europe to overcome the inefficiencies produced by the current national economic governance
of Europe-wide integrated markets. Silvio Pons' analysis of
Europe's relation to a potential strategic partner, Russia, sets the
endpoint to this collection of essays.

This book touches on many points associated with the debate
about a 'Social Europe'. The deliberations have however just
begun and are by no means comprehensive. If one thing is for
certain, it is that this topic will not disappear in the near future.
All European nations need to be involved in establishing a firm
European dimension of the ESM even if conflicting views are
unavoidable. Therefore we consciously invited authors from
eleven countries to write for this book guaranteeing maybe not
a unitary but an inclusive discussion. The debate about a 'Social
Europe' must be led in a broad way and also include the citizens
of Europe who rightly feel alienated by the current nature of
European integration. We must make sure that the legitimacy
and acceptance of the 'great adventure of Europe' matches its
political potential and significance.

References

Giddens, Anthony (2006): The World Does not Owe us a
Living! The Future of the European Social Model, in: Anthony
Giddens, Roger Liddle, Patrick Diamond (eds): Global Europe,
Social Europe, Cambridge.

From the Constitutionalisation of Europe to a European Constitution

By Peter Brandt and Dimitris Tsatsos

The Constitutionalisation of Europe – Historical Preconditions

The idea of a closer European Union, as a kind of league of princes and in sharp delineation from the Islamic Ottoman Empire and, to a lesser extent, also Russia and the Orthodox Eastern Church, began to find expression from as early as the 15th century in plans for a confederation put forward by rulers such as Henry IV of France. Beyond that, and usually more vaguely, eminent thinkers such as Johann Amos Comenius, Jean Jacques Rousseau and Immanuel Kant articulated the idea of European unity. Henri Saint-Simon, also one of the early utopian socialists, envisaged all of Europe as a constitutional monarchy with a bicameral parliament. Conservatives like François René Chateaubriand developed their own visions, as did representatives of the liberal-democratic national movements, for example Giuseppe Mazzini , the bourgeois peace movement and of course socialism in all its currents. Indeed the differentiation of the large cultural and social space west of the Urals into

9

modern nations is a typically European phenomenon. The SPD, for instance, in its Heidelberg Programme of 1925 advanced the slogan of 'United States of Europe'.

It was at this time, under the shadows of the First World War, that the idea of European unification began to play a larger role in realpolitik terms. In 1930 Aristide Briand, then France's left-liberal foreign minister, first presented other governments with his plan for a European federation, inspired by the pan-European movement of Count Richard Coudenhove-Calergi. Due to the beginning world economic crisis and the protection-ist measures taken by nation states on the one hand, and the unbroken traditions of national power politics and the corre-sponding thought patterns of all involved on the other, Briand's plan did not progress beyond initial discussions.

A decisive turning point was reached with the Second World War, when the larger part of the European continent was occu-pied by Hitler's Germany, which attempted to unite a fascist Europe under its own leadership. In all the occupied countries the heads of the resistance, from the national-conservative to the social democratic-socialist wing (but with the exception of the communists), formulated the programmatic demand for a European unity that appeared essential for security and eco-nomic reasons. Only by overcoming traditional power politics and unrestricted national sovereignty in favour of a suprana-tional federal authority would Europe and the nations contained within such a European Union be able to assert themselves against the new world powers.

Social democrats in particular saw the goal of establishing Europe as a 'third force' between the USA and the Soviet Union - not least in terms of its social order - as part of the unification perspective. This lost all chance of realisation when the British government, to which great hopes had been attached, refused to play the leadership role expected of it. In view of Stalin's brutal imposition of exploitation and conformity in the Soviet sphere of power on the one hand, and the determination of the US to uphold their economic and strategic interests on this side of the Atlantic on the other, a decidedly democratic-socialist policy of European independence was already faced with enormous obstacles. A 'Socialist Movement for the United States of Europe', founded in June 1947, could not expand this narrow room for manoeuvre.

From as early as the late 1940s onwards, efforts at European unification, inevitably confined to western Europe, became an element in the East-West conflict and American hegemonism, although this began to change in parts from the 1960s. To begin with the USA clearly saw more advantages than risks in a closer union of Europe, with or without Great Britain, and unambiguously supported the early projects: from the coal and steel community via the (failed) European Defence Community with its concomitant unified political structures to the European Economic Community of the Six agreed in 1957.

The latter's gradual expansion into a union that was soon to incorporate almost all of non-Russian Europe, and its institutional consolidation, has from the beginning, and always anew, posed the kind of fundamental questions with which the unification process is still coming to grips and which inevitably stand at the centre of a 'European Constitution'. As a matter of fact, the unification process has always contained both intergovernmental and supranational elements, with the former usually dominant. Even De Gaulle however, with his attempt to bring the European communities under the control of a French-led confederation of states, could not and probably would not completely eliminate the supranational element.

In contrast, attempts to give the Constitution of Europe a predominantly federal character (such as the first one undertaken in 1962 in a draft written by an ad-hoc group for the governments) have so far failed due to the resistance of individual states. The Constitutional Treaty of 29th October 2004 is therefore characterised by above all the equal weight given to the two structural principles and its avoidance of any finality on this question while simultaneously keeping open the possibility of a further development of the Union - especially with regards to the powers of the Parliament, which have already been significantly expanded since the 1980s.

Historical Preconditions of the Constitutional State in Europe
The gradual emergence of a 'European Constitution' is unthinkable without the specific European tradition of the constitutional nation state, which itself builds on much older historical traditions. The basic principle of Europe's historical development since the Middle Ages is pluralism: between the variegated and relatively small-scale, and mostly aristocratic, units as well as within the various communities where the emerging processes of politics favoured functionally differentiated systems over autocracies. This characteristic 'pluralism' usually expressed itself in violent terms, in sometimes very bloody wars and civil wars which permeated European history and were only exceptionally interrupted by prolonged periods of peace. The military, war and power expansion, moreover, constituted one of the major forces behind the technological and economic formation of Europe until the middle of the twentieth century. The social hegemony of the nobility was based on a thousand years of dominance by the feudal agrarian mode of production. Complemented by cooperative elements of varying strengths in peasant communities, this limited the role of monarchies as agents of pre-modern state formation. It equally limited the relatively autonomous European towns and cities as centres of trade and commerce. The social and occupational differentiation in the medieval and early-modern city required a much higher level of regulation compared to rural society, this applied especially to law, administration and finance, and the necessity of involving a considerable number of people in political decisions.

The traditional autonomy rights of the nobility and the urban citizenry, combined with the early codification of property law, represented insuperable obstacles against an arbitrary and violent appropriation of surplus produce by the monarchs and required the participation of the 'estates'. The political assemblies of the estates were dominated almost everywhere by the nobility. Yet despite their social limitations they established a tradition of representation against the rulers which was important for the future constitutionalisation. Even in the epoch of 'absolute' monarchy – that is limited only by divine and natural law – and in the most 'absolutist' states the intermediary powers of the estates remained much more important than has been commonly assumed. The claims to autonomy and participation of the estates included, in certain conditions, the right of resistance to a law-breaking authority, perhaps even violent resistance. Modern declarations of human rights are grounded in the Europe-wide discourse of resistance in the early modern era.

One of the most fundamental historical preconditions of the constitutional state in Europe was the role of the Christian - especially Catholic - churches as a unifying factor in the ancient European political culture. The church had absorbed the cultural heritage of antiquity, including that of Roman law, which served to legitimate the monarchical central power arising in the late middle ages. There was no direct road from a feudal society based on legal inequality and territorially fragmented empires to a modern constitutional state which, while divided into socio-economic classes, required a citizenship defined by legal liberty and equality. It was only the rise of the sovereign state in the form of absolute monarchy during the 17th and 18th centuries which pushed back the intermediary powers of the estates to such an extent that a politically more uniform society of subjects came into existence, while on the opposite side the executive functions of the ruler became increasingly differentiated and transferred to the bureaucracy. The relationship between a society of subaltern subjects and the monarchical state power became both more direct and more abstract. Moreover, against the background of a social and economic dynamic which had been clearly accelerating since the mid 18th century, it demanded a new set of administrative and juridical rules.

Alongside the originally dominant medical and geographic uses of the word 'constitution' it was common to consider fundamental treaties and laws, such as the British Magna Carta of 1215 or the Roman-German 'Golden Bull' of 1356, as 'constitutional laws'. However, none of these 'constitutional laws' of the early modern period was intended to provide a comprehensive political framework; they were always concerned with pressing individual issues even if their settlement implied broader commitments. It was only the modern concept of a constitution which made possible the part revolutionary, part reformist transformations of the political systems of Europe around 1800. Examples included the 'constitutions' of the USA (1789), with its strong influence on Europe and France (first 1791, the same year as the Polish effort which was frustrated by the second and third partition). The beginnings of this modern concept of constitutions reach back to Britain in the early 17th century. They continued to take shape during the 18th century in the debates among the enlightened intellectual elites of the continent, acquiring an increasingly normative and political charge: individual freedom, equality before the law, division of powers, press freedom, political representation. Between the late 18th and the mid 20th centuries, in particular, one can identify broad, Europe-wide connections, certain waves and regions of constitutionalisation which strongly qualify the dominant image of this age as a long epoch of national fragmentation.

The first republican-democratic constitution had come into being as early as the 1750s under the special conditions of the Corsican secession from Genoa; the project finally failed in 1769 with the French annexation of the island. The highly developed plan by Archduke Peter Leopold, the later Emperor, for the constitutionalisation of Tuscany in the 1780s, too, did not come to fruition mainly because of the resistance of the conservative clergy. Yet it deserves study as a strong example of enlightened reform absolutism. The examples mentioned here show that the constitutional state was 'in the air' from the final quarter of the 18th century at the latest. They also point to the fact that the

long road from the early, usually monarchical, constitutionalism to a fully-fledged democracy was certainly not smooth or
without contradictions. Rather, it was marked by massive, even
violent, resistance and reactionary retrogressions, and in the
inter-war period even by a complete, albeit temporary, change
of direction.

The Constitutional State of the 19th Century

Important as the role of revolutionary France as part catalyst, part
direct promoter – via the Napoleonic hegemonial system – was
for the transformation of Europe around 1800, it could only play
this role because there had been for some time – more in some
places than in others – changes taking place in society and social
consciousness which alone made it possible for the revolutionary
impulses 'from the outside' to find fertile soil. Beginning with the
Spanish war of independence, the idea of the self-determination
of 'nations' made a dialectical turn against the Emperor, not least
as a result of constitutionalisation. The extent to which there was
a common and fundamental political transformation and paradig-
matic change all over Europe around 1800 was shown when the
so-called 'restoration' after Napoleon's defeat not only left most
of the important social and political reformations of the previous period untouched, at least in western, northern and central
Europe, but also permitted another wave of constitutionalisation
following the *Charte Constituionelle* of 1814, especially in the
south German states. It was the new bourgeois elites, the 'educated' in Germany, the *notables* in France and the 'middle classes' in
England (of whom only the latter represented anything like a real
bourgeoisie) who understood the constitutional state as a means
of its own emancipation and also, simultaneously, as a means
of integrating the post-revolutionary societies (if necessary, in
league with the monarchy). Alongside this moderate liberal constitutionalism, and in part opposed to it, could be found more
radical, more plebeian currents, which, usually in connection
with social protests, demanded the unrestricted sovereignty of
'the people' as was the case in the French Revolution after 1789.

Through decades of struggle within parliamentary bodies, in publishing and not least on the streets and often also in armed struggle, the liberal 'party of movement' achieved the constitutionalisation of all of Europe's states, culminating in the revolutionary events of the early 1830s and late 1840s. The foundation of new nation states in Italy (1859-61) and Germany (1866-71) as a result of, on the one hand, the bourgeois national and constitutional movement and, on the other, the military dominance of the states of Piedmont and Prussia, concluded this process in the main. The constitution, however, remained an exception, being imposed from above in Tsarist Russia as late as 1906, following the revolution of the previous year. Although it left the monarchical executive in a particularly strong position, it was none the less more than a mere pretence. The new nation states in eastern and southeastern Europe issued from the dissolution of the Ottoman Empire in the last third of the 19th century as well as from the destruction of Austria-Hungary and the eastward shift of Russia. The fact that these nation states were constitutional states from the start - at least on paper - was already considered normal.

It is well known that the constitutionalisation of England preceded that of continental Europe by at least a century. In 1688-89, following decades of conflict between the lower house of parliament and the king, including a civil war, a *de facto* constitutional monarchy emerged (the 'Glorious Revolution'). As they had done elsewhere, the financial prerogatives of parliament became the main lever of successive constitutional change. Although no comprehensive political framework law was ever adopted and no such law exists to the present day, a concept of 'the constitution' emerged. This comprised documents – some going back to the Middle Ages – stating the personal rights of the Englishman or Briton, such as the 1689 Bill of Rights, as well as the Common Law and the unwritten rules of constitutional practice. The result is an evolutionary, customary law-based understanding of constitution which has only recently begun to adopt elements of the more normative, systematic and judical concepts of the continental European countries (as well as the USA).

Britain's constitutional monarchy with its tendency towards parliamentarianism was an aristocratic form of rule and remained so to some extent until the House of Lords was effectively stripped of its powers in 1911. However, the English nobility had always been socially open to the commercial bourgeoisie as a result of the strict rules of primogeniture and had established close economic and political ties with it quite early. The political taming of the high nobility by the Crown and the economic de-feudalisation of aristocratic land ownership in the early modern age provide the most important keys to understanding the pioneering role of England in both the constitutionalisation and the capitalist industrialisation of Europe.

Until the First World War, the pan-European process of constitutionalisation proceeded largely within the limits of a constitutional monarchy in a narrower definition – a monarchy limited by law but with the executive remaining with the ruler or a government appointed by him. Even in the Prussian-German, as well as the Austrian-Hungarian constitutionalism with its characteristic emphasis on executive power, it is possible to discern in the years around 1900 a creeping constitutional change which strengthened the government against the crown. This simultaneously strengthened the position of the national parliaments – elected through a general male franchise since 1867/71 in Germany, 1907 in Austria – against the executive and federal organs of the state. However, the breakthrough to parliamentarisation had to await defeat in the First World War; it could then no longer prevent the revolutionary democratic rising of the people.

All over 19th century Europe, therefore, constitutional monarchies below the level of parliamentarism still dominated. When in 1906 the traditional autocracy was replaced by a very modest version of constitutional monarchy even in Tsarist Russia, France had already had a parliamentary republic based on a general male franchise for over three decades. In Northern Europe, the introduction of women's right to vote was imminent. However, even France, for all its revolutionary traditions, remained a monarchy between 1804 and 1870, with only a brief interruption. Switzerland, the only constant republican country in Europe, only became a modern federal state in 1847-48 and it was not until 1874 that a combination of parliamentary and referendum democracy established itself. Otherwise it is possible to speak of the adoption of a parliamentary form of government (*de facto*, not necessarily *de jure*) at this time only in Italy (1861), the Netherlands (1868), Norway (1884) and Denmark (1905), with some reservations also Greece (1875) and Serbia (1903); only Great Britain and Belgium had done so much earlier in the 1830s and early 1840s if one ignores the special case of a temporary, quasi-parliamentary government by the French ultra-conservatives under the Bourbon monarchy restored in 1814.

The European constitutional state of the 19th century and beyond, of course, organised a capitalist class society founded upon extreme inequality, which in addition was marked by a mixture of many pre-bourgeois and clientilist elements. The representative organs even of established parliamentary states such as Britain were elected on the basis of (initially very) restricted and unequal franchises. In addition, it is important to emphasise the fundamentally manipulative character of European constitutional development. This applies not only to the southern and south-eastern periphery of the continent but also to the plebiscitary-populist Bonapartism of the two Napoleons, as well as to the specific lobbyism of sectoral interests in Imperial Germany. The Spanish *turno pacifico*, in which governments were changed by arrangement between the conservatives and liberals and only subsequently legitimised through systematic electoral manipulation and falsification, was matched by the Italian *transformismo*, a veritable system of oligarchic rule by a liberal government elite in which local clan chiefs and the leaders of provincial administrations took care of the desired results. In Italy as in Spain, where the Constitution of Cadiz (1812) had provided one of the early examples of relatively far-reaching constitutionalism, such practices led to a thorough discreditation of parliamentarism; much the same can be said for the corruption and clientelism inherent in the constitutional practices of the Balkan states.

From the Liberal Constitutional State to Social Democracy

The rising democracy movement in many European states around 1900 demanded, alongside the strengthening of parliaments, above all improvements in the franchise. In Britain, through a series of extensions – in 1832, 1868, 1884, 1918 and 1928 – the general franchise for men and later also for women was gradually achieved. The demand for a democratic franchise, fought for bitterly with mass demonstrations and strikes, was a key issue for the young socialist workers' movement which considered parliamentary democracy, preferably in the form of a republic, as the most beneficial form of government in a bourgeois-capitalist society, but also at the same time as the form of its abolition. Alongside the labour movement, and sometimes in alliance with it, were the radical liberal currents of the bourgeoisie and petty bourgeoisie, and sometimes also the peasantry. This contributed to the achievement of democratisation against the traditional ruling elites of the aristocracy and big bourgeoisie.

This phase of the democratisation of the franchise and, where it was still unachieved the parliamentarisation of government, corresponded also with the era in which the legal regulation of social policy became a political issue. Here too this occurred with the involvement of bourgeois politicians who recognised the need to secure the working population against existential risks such as accidents, illness, old age, later also unemployment. The pioneering model was the social insurance system introduced in the 1880s for the German Empire by the conservative chancellor Otto von Bismarck. Even though Bismarck's motives were patriarchal and anti-socialist and the material benefits quite modest in the beginning, social security and the improvement of employment law gradually became a constitutive element of the European constitutional and democratic model. The difference between financing social security through taxes or contributions is, in this context, secondary.

The expansion of social security systems with regards to their objects, expenditures, performances and the number of those insured to the concept of the 'social state' or 'welfare state' occurred after the Second World War. It was made possible by the long phase of reconstruction and prosperity, the East-West conflict and the temporary, and in some countries more long-term, dominance of social democracy and Keynesian economic policies. It would not be much of an oversimplification to say that – Great Britain apart – democracy did not reach the degree of stability required for the process of European unification in western Europe until the 1950s. The welfare state element in the political order must be considered the most important precondition alongside the defeat of fascism and its collaborators.

After the First World War, during the Weimar Republic, political theorists and constitutional law experts from the ranks of German social democracy, especially Hermann Heller, had argued that the 'material' or 'social' law-based state, as it found expression in the articles of the Weimar constitution concerned with labour and social policy which themselves were a compromise between the republican bourgeoisie and the reformist labour movement, would expand the traditional legal and constitutional state by a qualitatively new dimension. The aim of social democracy and the trade unions was to gradually expand this dimension with their social policies and 'economic democracy' approach. It was thought that, in legal terms, it would even be possible to overcome capitalism and realise socialism without any change in the text of the constitution and without leaving the territory of representative democracy.

The key argument was that without a minimum of 'social homogeneity' – which, under the conditions of market capitalism, included also the ability to achieve compromise between different interests on the basis of consensual notions of justice – the masses could not be enabled to complete the self-determination of the people in actual political practice and therefore could not become an integrated citizenry.

These still very relevant deliberations on constitutional policy were directed not only against the old liberal idea that formal freedom and equality before the law were sufficient. They also entailed a clear contrast with communist statism with its political dictatorship, abolition of the division of powers and fully nationalised command economy, as it had then taken shape in Russia and would later be exported to many regions of Europe and Asia. The theory and practice of a radical-democratic council system as the political form of socialism, which had emerged in several variants from the revolutionary upheavals of 1917-18, had in Russia been overlaid from the start by the educational dictatorship of the Bolshevik party elite. The end of that system in the east European popular revolutions of 1989-91 can therefore also be understood as a constitutional revolution.

The European Constitution – the Politicisation of the Process of European Unification

The aforementioned historical procedure, i.e. the route of the constitutionalisation process in Europe, defines and renders the course towards a European Constitution. That is, the historical procedure of a *lato sensu* European constitutionalisation acquires a concrete form through the creation of the European Communities in 1952 and reaches its first peak and a temporary 'integration' with the signing of the 'Treaty establishing a Constitution for Europe' on 29th October 2004.

The history of the idea of the European Constitution, which commences with the concept of the constitution of the nation state, evolved and adapted to the idea of a transnational, supranational and at the same time multinational legal order of states. The term 'constitution' – irrespective of the accuracy of the term for describing the European Constitutional Treaty – refers, even symbolically, to the political will to create a unitary legal order or, in any case, a common legal framework of competencies, to ensure a space of liberty. This might be the problem of the constitutionalisation of the integration process – to create for the European Union a state-like quality.

These elements are the starting point and constitute historical and logical conditions for the unification course: a transition from an international law nature to an institutional condensation and, finally, the outcome of a constitutional law nature. The history of the concept and meaning of 'constitution' in Europe explains a constitutional romanticism, which has prevailed in the European Union and gave rise to the will and the dynamic of its respective evolutions. The international law nature of the Communities rendered them inappropriate for a constitution. The legal-political content of unification however, its rationale, already incorporated all the elements of constitutional necessity.

**The Development of European
Integration into a Political Process**
The contemporary history of European integration has as a symbolic starting point: 9th May 1950, which is nowadays celebrated as 'Day of Europe'. At that time, the French Minister of Foreign Affairs Robert Schuman proposed the establishment of a supranational organisation for the common administration of two principle sectors of economic policy, coal and steel. His final objective was to ensure peace and prosperity in post-war Europe through solid cooperation links between the European states, especially between Germany and France. In 1952, the European Coal and Steel Community was established (ECSC) with the participation of six European states: France, Germany, Italy, The Netherlands, Belgium and Luxemburg. The undertaking of ECSC proved to be so successful that some years later the six states decided to extend their cooperation to even more sectors. In 1958, two additional communities were established through the Conventions of Rome, which were signed in 1957: the European Economic Community (EEC) and the European Atomic Energy Community (EAEC).

The European Communities have been based since the beginning on a novel principle of transnational cooperation, which went beyond the concept of a traditional international organisation. The core of the unifying task lay in the so-called 'community method' of cooperation which was based on the transfer of sovereign rights from the member states to the Communities, as well as on their joint administration at European level. Schematically: the Council, where representatives of member states participate, decides, the Commission proposes to the Council and implements its decisions, while the Assembly, which was composed at that time by representatives of the national parliaments, had an advisory role.

The European Communities evolved into a pole of attraction for the remainder of the states of western Europe: in 1972 Great Britain, Denmark and Ireland joined, in 1981 Greece and in 1986 Spain and Portugal. The last enlargement was accompanied by the first revision of the founding treaties, under the Single European Act in 1986. This historical moment marks the evident commencement of politicisation of the phenomenon of the Union. On the basis of the Single European Act, a decision to create a unified internal market was made and the first step was taken towards the political – apart from economic – unification of Europe, through the establishment of a mechanism of loose coordination of the external policy of member states, the European political cooperation.

The European Unification Process Undergoes
a First Institutional Deepening

At the end of the 1980s, while the existing socialist regimes were collapsing and the reunification of Germany was becoming a reality, everybody realised the need for deepening not only the economic unification but also the political unification of Europe. Moreover, the unified internal market in 1992 created the conditions – and according to many the need – for a single currency. In 1991, the Maastricht Treaty was signed, according to which the European Union was established as it principally operates to date. The European Union is based on three pillars. The first pillar refers to the European Communities, where the community method is implemented. An underlying evolution was the creation of the Economic and Monetary Union (EMU), which was completed on 1st January 2002 with the circulation of the Euro. The second pillar refers to Common Foreign and Security Policy (CFSP), where cooperation in the field of external policy is implemented at intergovernmental level. The third pillar, finally, refers to cooperation on issues of justice and home affairs (e.g. asylum and migration policy), where the member states cooperate also at intergovernmental level, i.e. without the community method being implemented.

Amsterdam

Following the enlargement of the European Union in 1995 (Sweden, Finland and Austria) a third revision of the treaties took place under the Amsterdam Treaty in 1997. This treaty extended the implementation of the Community method of cooperation and enriched the institutional framework of CFSP; however the problem of preparing the Union – and especially its institutions – for an already visible enlargement of the European Union towards eastern Europe was not dealt with. This task was undertaken by the next intergovernmental conference for the revision of the treaties, which lead to the Treaty of Nice.

Nice

By means of the Treaty of Nice (2000) the Union attempted to solve the leftovers of the Amsterdam Treaty and to render the Union capable of receiving the twelve member states that were in the course of accession negotiations. Among the achievements of the Treaty of Nice were the promotion of the community method in new policy sectors, the reinforcement of the European Parliament and the facilitation of enhanced forms of cooperation. It remains to be seen though, since these forms of cooperation have not been used so far, whether they will serve the need for flexibility or whether they will endanger the unity of the European Union in the future.

In parallel, a compromise in the institutional architecture of the enlarged Union was achieved: the composition of the Commission and the Parliament in a Union of 27 was regulated and the votes for decision-making in the Council were allocated. The Charter of Fundamental Rights that was elaborated by a Convention established for this purpose was not incorporated into the Treaty, despite the efforts of the European Parliament, but was adopted as a political declaration. The Treaty of Nice was enforced on 1st February 2003 paving the way for the enlargement of the EU. As of 1st May 2004 Estonia, Cyprus, Malta, Latvia, Lithuania, Hungary, Poland, Slovakia, Slovenia and the Czech Republic became members of the Union. The Treaty of Nice constituted a difficult compromise, which was not convincing as a basis for the future of the enlarged Union. In particular the solution of weighted votes has since the beginning been considered extremely complex, partly unfair, and convoluted for citizens. The allocation of competencies between the member states and the Union, the role of national parliaments, the incorporation of the Charter in the Treaty, as well as the overall rationalisation and simplification of the treaties, could not be achieved in Nice.

The Necessity of a Constitution Becomes Directly Visible
A crucial point of the institutional evolution of the European Union is that Nice determined *expressis verbis*, in a declaration annexed to the Treaty, the limits of the intergovernmental conference as a method for the revision of treaties: lack of transparency and publicity created intense alienation of the European citizens from the procedure of European integration. Thus, during the Nice Summit in December 2000 the member states decided to embark on a new attempt for global dialogue on the future of Europe. A year later, during the Laeken Summit (December 2001) the European Council decided to convene a new unofficial organ, the European Convention for the Future of Europe, following the successful example of the convention that elaborated the Charter of Fundamental Rights; the objective of the convention was to prepare the subsequent intergovernmental conference.

The Convention

The mandate of the European Council to the Convention was to elaborate proposals in three directions, namely how to bring citizens closer to the endeavour of European unification and to European institutions, how to organise politically the enlarged European Union in order to operate efficiently, and how to ensure a reinforced role for the Union in the world. At the same time, the Convention had to examine whether the need to simplify the treaties could be served by the adoption of a constitutional text. The Convention was composed of 16 representatives of the European Parliament, a representative of the government of each member state and two representatives of each national parliament. The representatives of the ten accession member states had equal status, while the candidate countries (Romania, Bulgaria and Turkey) were given observer status. Two members of the Commission and – under observer status – representatives of the Economic and Social Committee, of the Committee of the Regions, of the European Ombudsman and the Court of Justice of the European Communities, participated.

The works of the Convention were initiated under the presidency of Valery Giscard d'Estaing in February 2002 and were completed in June 2003. It operated under conditions of unprecedented publicity and transparency for European standards. Within the limits of the possible, the Convention set the conditions for the expression and participation of civil society and elaborated ideas for almost all the provisions of the European treaties. During its operation, the Convention acquired a reinforced political dynamic, which led the governments of many member states to have representation at the level of ministers of foreign affairs. Under the guidance of the steering committee, the Convention finally managed to surpass the initial mandate of the European Council; instead of being restricted to the submission of different alternative proposals, it drafted a global, and to a large extent novel, comprehensive 'Draft Treaty Establishing a Constitution for Europe' which was adopted on 13th June 2003 with consensus. The draft treaty was submitted to the Thessaloniki Summit on 20th June, which adopted it, despite the objections of several member states, as a solid basis for the works of the intergovernmental conference.

The European Constitution
The intergovernmental conference was initiated in October 2003 in Rome under the coordination of the Italian presidency. The objective of the presidency, supported mainly by Germany and France, was to decrease the spectrum of issues to be discussed anew. In that way, two tendencies were formed: the first was the position of the countries which supported the draft of the Convention or pursued limited improvements and amendments; among them was also Greece. The second tendency was expressed by countries which adopted a critical stance towards the draft of the Convention and maintained that it had proceeded with the unification endeavour (especially Great Britain) or that it was impairing their interests (especially Spain and Poland). The effort to conclude the conference in December 2003 failed, since it proved impossible to achieve unanimity among the 25. It should be highlighted that the consensus of the ten new member states was deemed necessary, although they were not yet formally members of the European Union. A key issue of disagreement was the refusal of Spain and Poland to accept the Convention's proposal regarding decision-making at the Council and their insistence on the maintenance of the Nice system, which almost put them level with the four bigger member states.

   The endeavour was further taken up by the Irish presidency, which reevaluated the new political conditions created by the fall of the governments of Aznar and Miller in Spain and Poland respectively, and convened anew the intergovernmental conference in April 2004. The Irish presidency was based on the *acquis* of the first phase of the intergovernmental conference and attempted to reduce the number of issues under negotiation, despite the efforts of some member states (especially Great Britain's) to 're-open' several topics. Following a complex compromise on the critical issues, the 'Treaty Establishing a Constitution for Europe' was finally approved by the intergovernmental conference, namely, by all the member states, that convened at the European Council, held in Brussels on 17th and 18th June 2004. The 'Treaty Establishing a Constitution for Europe' was signed by the governments of the member states on 29th October 2004 in Rome, following the necessary technical elaboration of the final text and its translation into all official languages of the Union.

Should one fact be designated as the main starting point of the last phase of constitutionalisation of the Union, this is beyond any doubt the enlargement, which cannot be compared to the previous ones neither quantitatively nor qualitatively. The leap of the Union from the 15 of the European west (and south) to the soon-to-be 27 of the reunified continent, was the catalyst, which accelerated evolutions and overcame the existing objections.

With respect to the method, the procedure of the intergovernmental conference served the six founding members and reached its limits with 15 members. However, it was made clear that it would possibly not continue to endure – as an exclusive procedure – with 27 members.

The content, form, structure and decision-making procedures foreseen by the treaties were planned for six member states and operated in a relatively satisfactory way, with minor amendments, for 15 members as well. However, it was certain that a Union with 27 member states would be condemned to paralysis. To sum it up, the historic events of 1989 politically imposed the enlargement. The enlargement politically imposed the Constitution.

Constitution or Constitutional Treaty?

The term 'constitution' has a specific history in continental Europe and therefore a specific content. Firstly, the Constitution emanates from procedures based on increased legitimisation. Secondly, the Constitution has acquired, through the evolution of European institutional culture, a specific content and includes regulations of a specific nature. The first prerequisite – the constitution-making procedure – is not met, since the origin of its legitimisation is the international treaty concluded by the member states of the European Union. The fact that the Convention was set up brought about a certain constitution-alisation of the procedure, which is however not sufficient. The content of the European 'Constitution' undoubtedly has elements of constitutional quality. For these reasons the term 'European Constitutional Treaty' is more precise.

Final Remarks

The rejection of the Constitutional Treaty by a significant part of the European Left is justified in terms of opposition to neo-liberal ideology and capitalist globalisation. What must be criticised is not this basic political stance but the conclusion derived from it – that is, to consider the failure of the Constitutional Treaty and therefore the maintenance of the status quo as the lesser evil. The Constitutional Treaty is a step which can be taken in order to progressively expand the ability of the European Union to act and therefore also to provide the institutional framework for a defence of the welfare state model and the re-regulation of the capitalist economy. Whether or not that can be achieved will be decided by political conflict. The rejection of the Constitutional Treaty in France and the Netherlands however casts fundamental doubts on the Treaty's future.

References

Beyme, Klaus von (1970): Die parlamentarischen Regierungssysteme in Europa, Munich.

Brandt, Peter, Martin Kirsch, Arthur Schlegelmilch (eds) (2006 sq.): Handbuch der europäischen Verfassungsgeschichte im 19. Jahrhundert, Bonn.

British Management Data Foundation (2004): The European Constitution in Perspective. Analysis and Review of 'The Treaty Establishing a Constitution for Europe', Bruges.

Dippel, Horst (ed) (2005 sq.): Verfassungen der Welt vom späten 18. Jahrhundert bis Mitte des 19. Jahrhunderts. Quellen zur Herausbildung des modernen Konstitutionalismus, München.

Dippel, Horst (2002): Verfassungen der Welt 1850 bis zur Gegenwart, Munich.

Dobson, Lynn, Andreas Follesdal (2004): Political Theory and the European Constitution, London.

Fenske, Hans (2001): Der moderne Verfassungsstaat. Eine vergleichende Geschichte von der Entstehung bis zum 20. Jahrhundert, Paderborn.

Gillingham, John (2003): European Integration 1950 – 2003, Cambridge.

Häberle, Peter (2005): Europäische Verfassungslehre, Baden-Baden.

Heller, Hermann (1971): Gesammelte Schriften, Leiden.

Herzog, Roman, Stephan Hobe (2004): Die Europäische Union auf dem Weg zum verfassten Staatenverbund. Perspektiven der europäischen Verfassungsordnung, Munich.

Howe, Martin (2003): A Constitution for Europe, London.

Lipgens, Walter, Wilfried Loth (eds) (1985-1991): Documents of History of European Integration, 4 vol., Berlin, New York.

Mann, Michael (1986, 1993): The Sources of Social Power, 2 vol., Cambridge.

Maurer, Andreas, Simon Schunz (2003): Auf dem Weg zum Verfassungsvertrag – Der Entwurf einer Europäischen Verfassung in der Regierungskonferenz, Berlin.

Meyer, Thomas (2005): Theorie der Sozialen Demokratie, Wiesbaden.

Möstl, Markus (2005): Verfassung für Europa. Einführung und Kommentierung mit vollständigem Verfassungstext, Munich.

Reinhard, Wolfgang (1999): Geschichte der Staatsgewalt. Eine vergleichende Verfassungsgeschichte Europas von den Anfängen bis zur Gegenwart, Munich.

Ritter, Gerhard A. (1991): Der Sozialstaat. Entstehung und Entwicklung im internationalen Vergleich, Munich.

Schulze, Hagen (1994): Staat und Nation in der europäischen Geschichte, Munich.

Streinz, Rudolf, Christoph Ohler, Christoph Herrmann (2005): Die neue Verfassung für Europa – Einführung mit Synopse, Munich.

Walter-Hallstein Institut für Europäisches Verfassungsrecht (ed) (2005): Ein Verfassungsentwurf für die EU: Vom Konvent zur Regierungskonferenz, Baden-Baden.

The Future of Europe

By Giuliano Amato

For those who are mindful not of the past but of the future
of Europe, old and outdated issues, much more ideological
than real, should not be a matter of further concern. The duel
between the European federalists and the strenuous opponents
of the European 'superstate' has nothing to do with the challenges ahead of us. The European Union (EU) is increasingly
taking the shape of what I call the hermaphrodite of the new
times, in other words the shape of those organisations that
have been blurring the border between international agencies
and constitutional ones by adopting the organisational patterns
of both. Such a hermaphrodite responds to the needs and the
demands of the globalised world, by definition a world where
not just states but also individual persons are active supranational actors. For reasons due to our peculiar history, our Union
happens to be the frontrunner of these new patterns. And it is
in this context it has to be read, not in the context and with the
eyes of the past.

Since its early years Europe has always been marked by this double nature. Even though it was conceived as an international organisation, creating rights and obligations of the undersigning member states, it was given the power to adopt regulations directly affecting individual citizens. And already in the early 1960s the European Court of Justice read the clauses of the Treaty as the sources of individual rights on the basis of which citizens could challenge the actions or omissions of their nation states. The mixed nature of Europe was therefore visible even in these initial features.

It became more and more so with the direct election of the European Parliament, which had previously been an assembly of representatives of our national parliaments, only empowered to give its advice to the ministers of the member states, sitting in council and deciding upon the binding acts of the Community. Once directly elected, the European Parliament had the same expectations as the national parliaments with which it shared the same democratic legitimacy. On the one side it gradually moved from advice to co-decision in the legislative process. On the other side it increasingly looked at the Commission as the 'executive', politically responsible to the Parliament itself. At that point the Commission became a hybrid institution, for it retained its original nature as a technical agency at the service of the member states, but it also became that kind of 'executive' subject to a (political) vote of confidence of the Parliament both to initiate its activity and to remain in power.

I could quote several other aspects of the European Community that offer further evidence of it being a continuous hybridisation of principles of international and constitutional law: the primacy of community law, which is based on the Treaty but also on the constitutions (or on the parliamentary acts) of our national legal systems; or the discipline of the 'own resources', that despite them being 'own' are decided upon not only by the Council, but separately by our member states, which 'ratify' the acts of the Council (as if they were international agreements). However, it is in the developments which occurred after Maastricht that the hermaphroditic nature of our common architecture became mostly evident. In Maastricht the decision was taken that new missions should be jointly pursued by our member states, missions that were even more political than those directly connected with market integration (the main aim of the Community): a common foreign and security policy, judicial and police cooperation, a widening of the so-called 'Social Europe', the coordination of our economic policies mostly (but not necessarily) in connection with the creation of the Euro. Later on, with the Lisbon Agenda, also improving our overall competitiveness (and therefore education, research, industrial innovation etc.) was included as one of the European missions. During the negotiations that led to the Maastricht Treaty, the crucial question was raised of how to deal with the new missions: by transferring new and further regulatory competencies to the European Community (according to the community method), or by keeping such competencies at the national level and using the European level only to coordinate their exercise (according to the intergovernmental-cooperative method)?

The decision was taken not to transfer competencies and to develop, instead, sophisticated instruments (common indicators, benchmarks, peer review, recommendations to the states) that are exclusively and entirely 'cooperative', without any binding force. Upon this background a new cooperative Europe has grown up in parallel to the communitarian one, both with bridges and overlaps. In foreign and security policy political declarations of the Council have been supported through the use of Community instruments, namely economic sanctions towards third states, while in the field of immigration some of the cooperative missions have become communitarian (in other words, instead of coordinating their national competencies, our member states have passed them onto the Community). Also due to these bridges and overlaps, the overall construction has become hermaphroditic and the proposal of a double-hatted Foreign Minister (exercising the functions both of the High Representative of our Common Foreign and Security Policy (CFSP) and of the member of the Commission in charge of the Community's external relationships) is an eloquent image of it.

One might argue that this is much more a monster than a hermaphrodite, that hermaphrodites themselves cannot go very far and it would be much better for us to go back to the purity of the old models, eventually making our choice: a European international organisation, a European federation or a European superstate. But here comes my point. In our times there is nothing exceptional nor anomalous in us having a hermaphroditic organisation, for it responds to the needs and the patterns of a globalised world where the border between internal and international matters is not so clear cut or continuous as it used to be. Europe can rightly be considered the frontrunner in adopting these new patterns, but it is not the only organisation of states that has a legal reach going beyond the states themselves, directly affecting their citizens. International tribunals are another, though very circumscribed, example. And organisations such as the World Trade Organisation (WTO) and the International Labour Organisation (ILO), due to their current developments, can also be quoted as members of this expanding club.

It is a club already under the attention of several perceptive scholars, who are identifying the members of the club, and mostly Europe, as the prototypes of future governance; a new governance, they argue, based not on hierarchy but on cooperation, not on command but on dialogue, not on mutual exclusiveness but on mutual tolerance and understanding. Perhaps they go too far when they idealise these new patterns as a sort of paradise on Earth (I am thinking of the *European Dream* by Jeremy Rifkin who has, however, domestic American reasons for being so biased and benevolent towards Europe). In any event they are right when they point at our European architecture as a model of multilevel governance substantially relying on networking and using binding instruments only when needed to give the net the necessary strength.

Being so, there is no reason for us to go back to the old debates and therefore to the fight among the pure models of the past. On the contrary, what we should do is to pragmatically discuss how to make our network efficient. Europe has multi-level governance based on networking but there is no reason for us to fall in love with it in its current form, for it sometimes works, sometimes it does not. It is our responsibility to introduce the necessary corrections if the system fails. Nor do I see any difference between a British and a continental European in tackling this issue, for being British, I suppose, means not being ideologically in love with networking, but assessing obstacles and hindrances that might prevent our network from giving us a satisfactory level of delivery.

The European way to define the balance that is needed is expressed by our motto, 'united in diversity'. How much unity is needed vis-à-vis the diversities we want to preserve? How many of our diversities deserve to be upheld and how useful can our unity be in eliminating our unworthy diversities? In principle, the level and the instruments of unity will not necessarily remain the same if we widen the range of diversities to be preserved or we decide to eliminate some of them. And pragmatism, not ideology, is needed to cope with these issues.

Do we think that a European foreign policy is needed in a future world where the US and China are the only global actors and the UK, France and Germany become secondary and gregarious actors? If our answer is positive, we should convince our member states to increase the level of unity in this area and to correspondingly reduce national diversities. Do we think that religious, cultural and ethnic diversities should be at the core of our common richness and that none of them should prevail over the others? If our answer is positive, we should ask Europe just to preserve them, without going beyond the safeguard of equal rights for all. Do we think that social differences throughout Europe corrode the loyalty to the EU and therefore are not compatible with the positive image it needs among its own citizens? If our answer is positive, we should equip Europe with some essential instruments allowing it to promote the reduction of such differences in our national contexts.

And here I can finish, for the scope of my essay is accomplished. Looking at the future of Europe means being fine tuned firstly to the real nature of our common construction and secondly to the challenges ahead of us that can be more effectively and efficiently faced by using and improving it. I am aware I have limited myself to this preliminary work of fine tuning. But from here we can move towards a better and more convincingly supported future.

The Great Adventure of Europe

By Detlev Albers

'United in Diversity'

Whenever constitutions set out to establish their principles, there is usually no lack of grand ambitions involved in this process. Accordingly, the preamble of the European Constitutional Treaty calls on the continent's citizens to continue the 'great adventure' of their unification 'with due regard for the rights of each individual and in awareness of their responsibilities towards future generations and the Earth'. Over eighty years ago the German social democrats, in their Heidelberg programme, demanded, no less ambitiously, 'the formation of the United States of Europe'. This was supposed to be not merely in the interests of the European nations but also 'to achieve the common interest of all peoples in all continents'.

Both claims, the principle of sustainability with regard to future generations and the future of the Earth in general, and the common interest of citizens everywhere, are indeed no small objectives for Europe's integration process. In any case, one is completely justified in labelling these goals as social democratic. Against this backdrop, it should be all the more worthwhile to critically evaluate the results of this process sixty years later.

'United in Diversity' – there has rarely been a slogan as applicable and crisp at the same time. If these words were describing the present, the 'great adventure of Europe' would have already been accomplished. As it is, however, it seems to remain our job to take it on as an imperative of the Constitution and try to assess its popular appeal. The statement could firstly be confirmed by the fact that there has rarely been a period in European history where two generations experienced fewer times of war. It would be overestimating the impact of the European integration process though if we claimed it was the sole reason for this. Such a version of events would also too easily play down the often terrifying effects of the Cold War – four decades that accounted for two thirds of this period. There is more substance to the view that the predominantly peaceful nature of the radical changes that were triggered by the fall of communism in eastern Europe from Berlin to Kiev was due in no small part to the attraction of 'Project Europe'.

However, one should be quick to point out that our European maxim is only just beginning to prove its worth. After all, who could seriously claim to know the full extent of the variety within today's Europe, an entity of 25 member states, faced with the task of unification? And who could be so presumptuous as to make predictions about the diversity in what will possibly become an even further enlarged European Union (EU) in the next decade, with 28, 30 or even 35 member states? One thing, however, is certain: drawing attention to such questions does not mean to challenge the validity of the maxim; on the contrary, it is merely to highlight the extent to which adventure, courage and incentive are equally involved in this.

The 'Monnet Method'
When asking about the heart of European integration, its internal motor, there is no way around the 'principle of communitisa-

tion'. It means the conscious and desired transfer of sovereignty from the national to the supranational, European level, which has initially involved only sections of legislation and has focused on economic matters. The systematic parcelling out of the seemingly indivisible nation statehood and the systematic use of this practice in favour of further transfer of competencies towards the 'upper level' – the so called 'spill-over effect' – is aptly described in Brussels as the 'Monnet Method', after its political inventor. The history of the Schuman Plan, the coal and steel union, the EEC and Euratom has been cited often enough. It remains an idly academic question to ask whether the Marshall Plan, as an initial trigger, or the Korean War, as a warning example, had more influence on the willingness to initiate the process of integration in the heart of (western) Europe. Without a doubt it decisively shortened Germany's path back to sovereignty, though Germany now has to share this sovereignty with its partners. In any case, both recent and previous German history from the old *Reich* via the *Deutscher Bund* (German confederation) and the *Zollverein* (customs union) to the *Bismarck-Reich*, can serve as points of reference about how to deal with the completely new federal division of responsibilities within the European communities. For the other players – especially France, after all a victorious former allied power in two world wars – this step marked a turning point whose consequences cannot be overestimated.

The advantages of the 'Monnet Method' were obvious to those in a devastated post-war Europe. It has proved its dynamism time and again since, culminating in the establishment of a common currency some decades later. Countries that pool their energy sector and arms industry (at the time in question coal and steel) under a European 'high authority', effectively rule out the possibility of wars among them. If the scope of the method is then widened to the extent that it comprises the member states' whole economic systems, it creates a vastly enlarged market. Naturally, such a process includes transitional periods and occasional setbacks. The advantages of the 'economies of scale' for domestic producers, however, will grow even further when the newly created internal market is protected with collective external tariffs. Then again, the result is a high grade of attraction between the domestic market and the other European neighbours and even beyond them. It is because of this dichotomy that the Community becomes confronted over and over again with the risky parallelism of enlargement and integration.

In the face of the great advantages of economic integration, some of the more negative sides are overlooked all too easily. However, it is because of these downsides that the above mentioned aims of the Constitutional Treaty have often become diluted to little more than empty rhetoric. Those whose predominant concern is the expansion of markets and unfettered competition should not be surprised when the European 'market economy' also spawns a 'market society'. Whoever constantly comes up with new ways of removing (internal) national borders will suddenly come to the conclusion that 'deregulation' might be the easiest – if not the only – possible form of sovereignty transfer. Neither democracy nor public participation is automatically included in it. The 'Monnet Method' has no inherent obligation to be in the public interest. The EU Commission's first plans for the 'services directive' and its persistent adherence to the principle of the country of origin, leading to dumping effects on the site of the supplier, once again made this point clear. Communitisation in itself retains as small a guarantee of internal diversity as it does an outward commitment to international solidarity, without even mentioning the principle of sustainability. On the other hand, all this does not contradict the method of integration. It demonstrates, however, the sheer amount of political action that is needed to endow this method with a social dimension.

Union, Association of States, the Europe of the Regions and Local Authorities

'If it is the case that tariffs for international trade are only the result of the political division of different states, then in turn it must also be the case that unification of these states to a free-trade area will also lead to one and the same political system.' We do not owe this insight to a dedicated follower of Jean Monnet in the 1950s. The phrase was in fact already used back in 1829, in the run-up to the German customs union (*Zollverein*), by the then liberal Prussian finance minister Friedrich von Motz. It was expressed then with laconic words what would become, one and a half centuries later, the decisive theme of the 'European adventure': what is the most adequate form of statehood, of democracy and of a society based on social justice that, in the truest sense of the word, will have to be invented if one wants to continue to ride the 'tiger of integration'?

In the era of globalisation, old arguments from the early stages of the European Economic Community (EEC), such as the debate between the advocates of a 'confederation of states' and those of one 'federal state', were already confined to history a long time ago. Who would nowadays seriously advocate Charles de Gaulle's concept of the 'Europe of the fatherlands' or give more than a brief nostalgic thought to Margaret Thatcher's ideas about confederation? The German constitutional court's interpretation of the Maastricht Treaty, regarding it as an 'association of states' in the sense of a not yet defined blend somewhere between confederation and federation, was quite rightly perceived as a mere way of appeasing the group of Eurosceptics. In contrast to this view, particularly Anglo-American authors such as Stephen Haseler and Jeremy Rifkin, who have been able to preserve their outside perspective on the EU, have been debating the question as to whether Europe has already developed into a superstate, or more precisely, a second superstate along with the USA.

What, then, is the state of play regarding the EU's path to 'one and the same political system'? The economic sphere has been ahead of developments; this can hardly come as a surprise. As a consequence, monetary union has legitimately been criticised for the Euro being a 'currency without a state' (Padoa-Schioppa 2000) and therefore not robust. Nevertheless, it must be admitted that the development of the political system has almost

43

caught up with the development of the economic system. This certainly applies to the additional and altered chapters of the Rome Treaty, from the Single European Act, up to Nice, the Constitutional Treaty and of course the Brussels *acquis communautaire* collection of secondary European law. In the wake of the recent accession negotiations, experts have attested that the *acquis* constitutes a volume of more than 90,000 printed pages. The European institutional structure, with its specific balance of powers along with the growing influence of the Parliament as well as the principle of united democratic and basic social rights, has been widely acknowledged. In addition to this, however, genuinely new concepts are needed in all those areas where the continental design of the Union demands new and innovative solutions. As is demonstrated by the examples of multi-level democracy structures and the formulation of the subsidiarity principle, such new approaches regularly feature among the most controversial elements of the new European state.

The development of an effective and participatory democracy that works on multiple levels is without a doubt one of the most important institutional components of the European experiment. Its successful implementation has become more important with each expansion of the Union, necessary for the EU to counterbalance the centrifugal forces in today's Community which already comprises more than 450 million Europeans. For the numerous smaller member states it is about emancipating themselves from the dominating influence of their larger neighbours by using their over-proportional share in the Brussels decision-making process. The larger nations also need a balancing mechanism in order to respond to their citizens' increasing feeling of powerlessness or even separatist tendencies that are triggered by an ever more complex Union. The results can be observed in the increased importance of the regions, autonomous areas, voivodships or *Länder* such as in Germany and Austria. Simultaneous to the growth of the EU itself, this development is taking place in all of the larger member states. Only when the Brussels model of Europe is able to present itself as the Europe of citizens – via the Europe of the regions and that of the self-assured local communities – when it, moreover, manages to achieve a transparent and conclusive system of power sharing that devises an adequate and independent scope for action at every level, only then will the quantitative growth of the union go hand in hand with an increased internal cohesion. The principle of subsidiarity, i.e. the allocation of as much power as possible to the lower institutional levels, is a fundamental manifestation of this belief and was first embodied in Maastricht and later reaffirmed by the Constitutional Treaty. Everyone knows, however, that this can only be a very general indicator of direction. And it would be dangerous to hope for more precise indicators only from the existing institutions such as the Committee of the Regions (COR) alone.

The greater the number of states that are united within the Union, the more important it will become to establish a bottom-up process of democracy and to rise above a mere executive form of federalism. An indispensable condition for this process is a common form of action at all levels – including the European level – by all political and social stakeholders. This applies to political parties, trade unions and economic, environmental and consumer groups, as well as the rapidly rising number of other non-governmental organisations. It is the only way to create a vibrant European public sphere that remains aware of the variety of all its parts. It is also the only path to create and maintain a general willingness to provide the funds necessary to reduce the massively increased regional disparities. Something that has become all the more urgent in the wake of eastern enlargement.

The European Model of Society

Ironically, for decades, European social policy has been limited to playing a mere bit-part role. The founding fathers of the European Coal and Steel Community (ECSC) and the EEC explicitly deemed it secondary to economic integration. Nowadays, in the first decade of the new century, the European model of society is a talking point of central importance. This is the case despite the indisputable fact that there are considerable differences between the social security systems in northern and southern Europe and even more with regard to the eastern accession countries. Nevertheless, the general congruence within Europe is striking when compared to the respective institutions in the USA or Japan and all the more so when compared to newly industrialised nations or even developing countries.

This can mainly be explained by the fact that the 15 original member states of the EU experienced a 'golden age' in the decades following the Second World War. It was an exceptionally long period of economic prosperity marked by hitherto unprecedented growth rates. Apart from the considerable increases in salaries, this development led to reliable protection against the significant risks of life such as poverty in old age, illness, accident, unemployment and the need for care. Although these achievements were not the result of coordinated efforts within the different member states, they did however take place more or less simultaneously in each country. Accordingly, the educational system experienced considerable improvements. Its strategic importance has become even more relevant in the course of the transition to the knowledge-based society, although one has to note that this development has also been strongly linked to economic interests. That said, the European model of society has never been limited to the welfare state. There has always been the additional goal, at least on the part of the trade unions as well as the political Left, to achieve an effective taming and control of the 'wolfish nature' of capitalism by expanding people's material security and rights of democratic participation.

Some countries such as France (traditionally) and Italy (on a rudimentary level) placed an emphasis on a strong state, dominated by the Left, which was expected to provide the decisive economic and social directives in cooperation with the social partners. This was the essence of the French concept of *Tripartisme*. In contrast, Germany for a long time pursued a different strategy. As early as the times of the Weimar Republic, there was an attempt to exert influence on the direction of economic decisions 'from within'. First with the help of the workers' councils and later by applying the concept of economic democracy (*Wirtschafsdemokratie*). The basic idea was to control economic decisions in such a way as to serve the public interest. This explains the continuing strong position of the German works councils (*Betriebsräte*) today and the particular weight that is given to the equal representation of workers on the boards of large companies. Incidentally, some basic ideas had in fact much in common with the British concept of the 'industrial democracy'.

In Sweden, for many years the social democratic role model country, the development took yet another turn. Here, the goal of the Swedish *Folke Hjem* (home for all) notion was approached from two sides. On the one hand, there was the exemplary and far-reaching development of social security measures, based on a conscious and universally accepted redistribution of national income. On the other hand, it depended on a particularly pronounced social presence of the trade unions, which actually considered themselves as the real *Landsorganisationen* (national organisations). For a time, it seemed that this system could also be supplemented by the establishment of a comprehensive scheme of capital formation in the hands of the employees, the so called Meidner Plan. Finally, it should be noted that after the enlargement, at least eight of the current member states enrich the EU's socio-political wealth of experience with their practical knowledge about communist state-ruled economies (and also the abandonment of this concept). In the same context, the former East Germany and future accession countries also have to be taken into account.

During the last three decades of the previous century it became more and more obvious that even the bigger European states did not have sufficient weight to steer the economic process. This was, for instance, exemplified by the German social democrats' decision under the chancellorship of Helmut Schmidt to refrain from fully implementing their *Orientierungsrahmen 1985* programme, although it had only been adopted in 1975. The French political Left, after the first two years of François Mitterand's presidency, did not act any differently despite their promises in the *programme commun*. It was then, if not before, that all community members were faced with a choice: either to find a new scope for action in a European context that would compensate for the loss of national influence, or to watch helplessly as they were gradually forced back into doing nothing more than defending the welfare state system and to see the European Social Model being gradually stripped of its democratic and participatory elements.

In March 2002, the European Council of Barcelona made a veiled attempt at an answer when it stated: 'The European Social Model is based on good economic performance, a high level of social security, high quality education and professional training, *and social dialogue*' (italics added by author). Even in times when the economic situation was good, and employment and the standard of education were high, one had to wonder whether there was already too much expected from the dialogue of the social partners or its French form, the *Tripartisme*. That must certainly have been the case in times of crisis, when there was scarcely any economic growth, but instead immense unemployment, insufficient training, intensified competition for industrial location and demographic problems that had to be dealt with after having waited too long to get to grips with them. The 'social dialogue', even in its most obligatory form, must still remain within the limits of a persuasive exercise. This is not to say, by all means, that the 'social dialogue' was not helpful in the resolution of social conflicts. In this context the Brussels Economic and Social Committee, including its 'third bank', which is open to all other non-governmental organisations, has built up a solid record of beneficial activities over the last decades. It would, however, go far beyond the capacity of the 'social dialogue' to serve as the single steering instrument for the economy.

The 'great adventure of Europe' has drawn its strength not least from the insight that the whole is greater than the sum of its parts. Finally, this verdict has also to be taken seriously with regard to European social politics. An economic power, or even superpower, cannot be tamed by allocating it less power than has already been given to the national framework. Quite the opposite is true: only if we manage to combine the different participatory elements as they have emerged within the different member states and, on the basis of this, develop a genuinely European central idea, only then can we hope to adequately offset economic integration with a democratic social model of equal status. This requires a combination of the French guidelines regarding the primacy of politics as expressed in the demand for a common European economic government, the German principle of workers' participation in the industrial decision-making process and the extensive socio-political presence of workers' organisations as given by the Swedish example. Of course, these elements cannot simply be added up. It is crucial that the convictions that underline these concepts are going to cross-fertilise and supplement each other. Furthermore, they will only be able to exert their influence fully if this process goes hand in hand with the coalescence of all the different social democratic and socialist parties, trade unions and their social partners, to real pan-European organisations.

European Globalisation

'I wish for a Europe that creates its own identity without feeling too much need to separate itself from others. Basically Europe, for me, is only tenable as a model for a liveable future world community.' This was recently expressed by Adolf Muschg, Swiss writer and former President of the Berlin Science Academy. In a nutshell, this phrase specifies both the ambition and legitimacy of the European project.

Whether the member states like it or not, whether they are aware of it or not, with the Euro, the enlargement and hopefully the Constitutional Treaty, the EU has become one of the key players on the global stage, politically and economically. Whatever Europe is going to succeed in, be it further integration and the catching-up process of those new members who are lagging behind or be it improving the quality of Europe's leading national economies, everything will have direct repercussions outside Europe. It will provoke emulation, methodically and as regards content, and will also promote non-hostile competition with others. However, at the same time, the logic of the international network, the core of all globalisation, demands that Europe cannot detach itself from the rest of the world. Whoever does outward business must also accept the input from the outside under fair conditions – or otherwise they will get caught in an endless downward spiral of violence and thereby ruin the central pledges of their own constitution.

A simple and often uncomfortable rule of international relations states that there is a direct relation between a country's size and its obligation towards others. Many of the smaller European nations, for long enough also the Federal Republic of Germany, had tried to avoid taking this responsibility by referring to their respective larger neighbours. Voices from the other side of the Atlantic claim with great vigour that, for decades, Europe had been profiting from a sort of free-rider mentality. Impatiently, but by and large accurately, it is insisted that nowadays no member of the EU can stand aside simply citing lack of influence.

In doing so, it is by the state of international affairs itself that Europe is called upon to articulate its interests – and this refers to the union as a whole rather than to the extended foreign policies of individual member states. Despite the national preferences that still exist, one will then quickly be able to establish a number of shared positions on particular issues. These include the decisive assertion of the belief in multilateral regimes, including negotiation networks, the strengthening of the United Nations and its reform on the basis of the report to Kofi Annan (*A Safer World*) and not least the disapproval of strategies of pre-emptive strikes, as those currently advocated by the Bush administration. Without doubt, this would also demand European contributions to the fight against terrorism and against the proliferation of weapons of mass destruction.

This is not enough though. The more the EU presents itself as a unified and jointly acting power on the international stage, the more it must insist on realising far-reaching changes with regard to the fight against poverty, sustainable development and the prevention of potential global dangers, such as climate change. It has long become apparent that taming capitalism in a socially beneficial way will fail if limited to a European level only. Without constituting intercontinental alliances, which on their part will have to depend on the support of their respective citizens and governments, no breakthrough will be achieved.

Europe certainly does not have to worry about a lack of attention or unwillingness to cooperate. The declaration of principles of the Socialist International (SI) decided in Sao Paulo in 2003 (*Governance in a Global World*) can be referred to as an example in this context. However, what resonance such alliances offered by Europe will find outside and how attractive this offer will be to others will depend decisively on the extent to which the EU is able to portray itself as 'the model for a liveable future world community'.

References

Haseler, Stephen (2004): Super-State. The new Europe and its Challenge to America, London.

Hobsbawm, Eric (1995): Das Zeitalter der Extreme. Weltgeschichte des 20. Jahrhunderts, Munich.

Kagan, Robert (2003): Macht und Ohnmacht. Amerika und Europa in der Neuen Weltordnung, New York, Munich.

Kaelble, Hartmut (1987): Auf dem Weg zu einer europäischen Gesellschaft. Eine Sozialgeschichte Westeuropas 1880-1980, Munich.

Loth, Wilfried (1996): Der Weg nach Europa, Göttingen.

Muschg, Adolf (2004): Ich beneide die Deutschen um ihre historische Lage, *Handelsblatt* 30/31. December.

Nipperdey, Thomas (1983): Deutsche Geschichte 1800-1866. Bürgerwelt und starker Staat, Munich.

Padoa-Schioppa, Tommaso (2000): Der Euro und die Politik; in: *Internationale Politik*, vol.55, no.8.

Rifkin, Jeremy (2004): Der europäische Traum. Die Vision einer leisen Supermacht, New York, Frankfurt.

Sozialistische Internationale (2003): Governance in einer globalen Gesellschaft, edited by Christoph Zöpel, Sao Paulo, Berlin.

Vereinte Nationen (2004): Eine sicherere Welt: Unsere gemeinsame Verantwortung. Bericht der Hochrangigen Gruppe für Bedrohungen, Herausforderungen und Wandel, New York.

The Consequences of 29th May 2005

By Elisabeth Guigou

The crisis of Europe today is fundamentally different from any other crisis that has slowed down the Union's progress so far. Until now, every single one of these crises, including the most severe ones such as the 'empty chair' crisis in the 1960s or that of the British rebate in the 1980s, had resulted from the shock of national interests. But with the French 'No' of 29th May and the Dutch one of 1st June 2005, it is now the European project itself that is in crisis. Two founding members of the European Community have expressed their mistrust of Europe as it is being built. The majority of these two countries' citizens do not understand very well where Europe is going. This is a crisis of meaning. Europeans do not really know what they want to do together any more. As long as the driving force behind the European project was to ensure peace, and then democracy, the objectives and the direction were clear. Now that both can be taken for granted, we need a new project if we are to give Europe a new meaning.

What did the French, and the Dutch after them, express when they refused to ratify the Draft Constitutional Treaty? Some of them expressed their general rejection of Europe, be it for nationalist reasons or because they reject the free-trade liberalism the European Union (EU) embodies in their eyes. People who reject the European construction in principle have always existed; their opposition is long-standing and manifested itself in France in the vote for the Maastricht Treaty. What is new in this vote is that many staunch supporters of the European process have voted against the Draft Constitutional Treaty. Some have done so because they were against enlargement, either the previous enlargement that led to the 25 country Europe, or the possible future accession of Turkey. Others fear the free-trade liberal or technocratic drift of the Union. The 'Bolkestein directive', which was discussed during the French debate, heightened the fears of social regression linked to Europe, even more so since few people understood the process that led to its elaboration. In other words, what was rejected is a certain obscure, incomprehensible, non-democratic way to build Europe. Without a project behind it, without a real desire to live together and to further the understanding between our countries, Europe has eventually been reduced, in the eyes of many, to a mere machine that produces complicated directives that give rise to incomprehensible debates between unknown institutions. The fear of an infinite enlargement has also played a significant part.

The Draft Constitutional Treaty paid the price of this image and of these fears. An arid, complex reading for everybody who was not completely up-to-date on European debates, it has not convinced the French of the real progress it made possible. It has, on the other hand, comforted them in the belief that Europe is something distant and incomprehensible. Another difficulty of this text is that it was presented as a constitution, which it was not: it was not produced by a constituent assembly and the member states had to ratify it separately. It also comprised a third part on Community policies, which had no reason to be in a constitution, and this helped to make it inaccessible.

Even if the other member states ratify the Treaty, it will be impossible to have the French vote on it a second time. There is so far no 'plan B', which would allow us to draft another text, on the horizon. It will therefore, I think, be necessary to start new negotiations, probably after 2007, when France will have a new President of the Republic – in the hope that the latter will be interested in the European Union.

It is up to us, in the meantime, to show that Europe can give itself a new project. To do this, we must first of all give ourselves a significant European budget that will allow us to enact concrete projects.

The structure of the budget must be changed to allow for future-oriented spendings. We must go on reducing the sums allocated to the Common Agricultural Policy (CAP), whose weight has already gone down from 70 per cent to 42 per cent of the Union's budget. We must accept the principle of limiting export grants, since they have a perverse effect on the economies of developing countries. Conversely, the sums invested in rural development and territorial planning and development will become more and more useful. And we must put a strong emphasis on research, as it is most important for our economic future.

Generally, we must also increase the budget. Our Union will only be able to realise its potential if it gives itself an ambitious budget in the future: the current one is insufficient if we want to both finance the common policies, particularly the cohesion policies, and successfully manage enlargement.

The EU can be successful again and we need to launch a few concrete projects that can be immediately understood by Europeans, for instance the project of a digital library, which binds together culture and new technologies. But we can also think about renewable energies: they start to be competitive as the price of petrol goes up. Aside from research on the hydrogen motor, we should develop a way to stock up these energies and, once again, such a project can only take place at the Union's level, not at that of states or private companies.

More generally, reinforced cooperation can also allow us to go further provided we see it not in terms of including or excluding particular member states, but as defined by its content: this logic is what made the success of the Schengen and Euro projects. Priority goes to reinforced cooperation on economic and monetary union issues, so that the Eurogroup can have more weight in its dealings with the European Central Bank (ECB).

Finally, the Commission should encourage and finance throughout the Union a number of debates on what Europeans want to do together as well as on the boundaries of the Union. Associations and European foundations have a central role to play in this matter.

Indeed, we will not be able to have a real political union as long as the boundaries of the EU are not defined. The strong, federal, integrated political union I call for has only meaning inside fixed geographical boundaries. For me, the Balkans, and Turkey (if the conditions are met), are meant to be a part of it. On the other hand, for Ukraine, Moldavia and Belarus (once this country becomes a democracy), the question of relations between the EU and Russia needs to be debated. Reaching an agreement on these issues will take time, probably years, but it is a question we can no longer avoid.

Defining the boundaries of the Union also implies a redefinition of our relationships with our eastern and southern neighbours that are not destined to access the EU (Russia, southern Mediterranean countries). The question of boundaries must be addressed not in terms of a 'Fortress Europe', but through the offer of a renovated partnership, which would be at the same time more generous economically and more demanding in terms of democracy and the fight against corruption. With Southern Mediterranean countries, this partnership should function on an equal representation basis and aim at the eventual creation of a Mediterranean world community.

How to Overcome the European Crisis?

By Massimo D'Alema

Europe is having a hard time. The results of the referendums in France and the Netherlands have hampered the European Constitution ratification process. Public opinion across European Union countries is increasingly less enthusiastic about Europe.

Many have interpreted this rejection as a reaction against enlargement; for some time the political debate has been dominated by the *plombier polonais*, the Polish plumber.

However, the real reasons are far more complicated. Fears that have completely different origins have resulted in opposition to Europe. In countries such as France, where massive immigration from Maghreb has raised tensions, the possible admission of Turkey to the European Union is perceived as a risk of Islam expanding ever further across Europe. Some feel that there has been a progressive reduction in fundamental social rights which is directly related to the European Union, whereas others fear a loss of national identity.

The tragedies of terrorism have fed and strengthened these fears, leading to new nationalistic policies. Moreover enlargement exposes the institutional weakness of the European Union (EU), underlining the inadequacy of its decision-making mechanisms. For instance, it is evident that a unanimous voting system cannot guarantee the governance of a 25 member Union, and maybe the European Union should have been more courageous by initiating an institutional revision before any enlargement. The enlargement process forces us to face the issue of external borders: the European Union cannot expand indefinitely, invading neighbouring continents, but hopefully these can benefit from integration too.

The expansion of Europe means the expansion of stability, peace, democracy, and respect for human rights. Turkey is a good example. It is proceeding towards respect for minorities' rights, rights for women, abolition of the death penalty and prohibition of torture. It has begun an extraordinary process of civilisation with the objective of entering the European Union. To make all this possible we have to create mechanisms that will enable certain countries (countries that are not even becoming members of the EU), to extend their relationship with Europe. This means building even stronger relationships, not just by making commercial treaties; and in doing so these countries will have the opportunity to benefit from the advantages of the European Union.

Currently, there is no intermediate level between full membership and the Association Treaty. If such a level existed it would enable a varying degree of relationships which would be extremely useful when facing situations such as the Balkans and the Middle East.

In the past, many have proposed the entrance of Israel into the European Union. I believe it would be better to focus on a special relationship between Europe and some countries in the region, for example Palestine, Jordan and Israel itself; this would also avoid further isolation of Israel. Europe would guarantee not only development and integration, but also security needs in the region. The model for this could be NATO and their 'Partnership for Peace' designed with the former Soviet Union countries. They have not become members of the EU but have built a stable cooperation with it in security matters.

Enlargement can be an opportunity to integrate countries and regions with a high growth rate, and by doing so contribute to the global development of the European Union. It might also be beneficial for our countries, as the results of companies which have invested in new markets have already demonstrated. We also need to ask why our citizens are so apprehensive about enlargement, and why public opinion has rejected the idea of a politically stronger Union. The roots of this crisis are twofold. The first occurred with the war in Iraq, with so many in Europe opposed to United States policy, Europe was not able to build a common position. It was unable to prevent the war or hold the United States to account. European public opinion lost its faith when tens of millions of citizens rallied for peace and the European Union appeared totally powerless. This is due to its internal divisions. At that time, the mechanism appeared totally ineffective.

The second reason for this crisis is the failure of the Lisbon strategy; the failed take-off of a policy that is still the most courageous reformist manifesto ever written in Europe. That document was the product of a Europe with 11 governments who were all centre-left orientated. It has remained a sort of dream book because neither the mechanisms nor necessary resources were ever defined: even that centre-left Europe was unable to make the required steps forward. The defeat of European reformism and the reason why a different political season followed afterwards is also obvious: it was the lack of courage in facing the European integration process.

Today these problems haunt us. When Tony Blair invites us to build a common defence policy and to move policies towards innovation, he is making a very important step, especially as the leader of a country that is historically prudent towards political integration of Europe. Now is the time to really measure Europe's political willingness to face up to the most sensitive issues.

A sizeable topic that Europe must face in the months to come is how to save the Constitution. It has not been unreasonable to reflect and suspend the ratification process for a while, as it was clear that a 'domino effect' rejection of the Constitution was likely. Anyway, while waiting to restart the process, it is sensible to allow those who feel the need for a greater level of unity to use the existing mechanism to achieve it. Today we can work towards the challenging project of enhanced cooperation, allowing groups of countries in the Union – within the framework of the European Union – to develop more intense integration on specific issues, as happened with the Euro. In order for the structure of the Union to remain intact it is necessary that developments take place strictly within the legal framework of the Union, allowing those who wish to take part to do so easily. It is evident that the first possible issue for enhanced cooperation will be an economic one.

There is need for a flexible use of the Stability Pact in order to facilitate a policy response to the economic crisis. This would be even more effective if applied together with great European investment programmes, which would be better than giving back to individual national governments higher margins of flexibility in the budget. Deficit spending does not solve the problem of European competitiveness; we need to invest in those issues that actually limit our competitiveness. First we need to address the low innovation rate and then work on a qualitative change in the European economy. The International Monetary Fund (IMF) says that the impact of the Chinese economy on a global level will make our manufacturing products less competitive, whilst increasing the global demand for qualified services, luxury goods and technological innovation. The most advanced countries that are in a position to face this demand will take the biggest advantage of this situation. China could be an advantage for us, if we courageously look at the desires of its consumers, around 200 million people becoming more and more oriented towards foreign goods. The problem with European competitiveness (and even more for Italy's) is the lack of renewal of its development model, resulting in the absence of investment in innovation and research. All of this could be much more effective if implemented through a European coordinated programme, rather than through national policies. The first big enhanced cooperation could be on those issues, starting in the Eurozone and focusing on the integration of taxes and budget policies.

A second key issue should be common defence, and therefore common foreign policy. The first group could be composed of the Saint Malo Pact countries: Great Britain, France and Germany (Italy could easily join them). Common defence policies not only mean decisions on a military level, but also integration of industrial and research policies. It is absurd that each European country invests in every single field of military specialisation. The result is enormous expenditure, without changing Europe's immeasurably inferior military and defence capabilities compared to the United States. Defence (and foreign policy) and economic policies are two sectors in which enhanced cooperation could develop. The founding countries could concentrate on projects of enhanced cooperation.

In future, if the opportunity arises, the Constitutional Treaty issue could also be reviewed. The required time for ratification could be extended until after the French presidential elections. It is of course very difficult for a weak government recently defeated to come back and face a referendum on the same issue. But it is reasonable to expect that a new President could ask the French people to vote on a 'lighter' version of the Treaty, without the technical elements – a Constitutional Treaty reduced to the first and second parts, essentially the principles of the Nice Charter and the basic rules for the functioning of the institutions. The most controversial parts will be cut out, the countries that have already ratified would not need to have another vote, while those who have not yet voted could be called to ratify a different text; without those sections which the 'No' supporters were focusing on. This could be a way to enable Europe to start afresh by 2007.

The European enhancement process could be restarted now, but we need the strength to face complicated issues and make courageous choices. To support the leaders who care for this, it is necessary for political and opinion movements to start cooperating and give a push to this process. It is necessary for European Left parties to play a major role and to convince their leaders of this challenge.

Danger for Europe

By Garrelt Duin and Martin Schwanholz
(with the assistance of Victoria Krummel)

In the next few years, German social democracy must reso-
lutely seek the further development of the social dimension of
European integration.

'Tired of globalisation' was the headline on the cover of *The
Economist* on 5th November 2005. This was a reflection of the
fact that, in the more highly developed economies at least,
the economic euphoria of recent years is visibly waning. The
dream – using new information and communications technologies, the free movement of goods and finance and the removal
of tariff and non-tariff barriers to trade to enhance people's prosperity – is leaving an increasingly stale aftertaste. The processes
universally known as globalisation are producing fear, not confidence, in people. In addition, more and more people in positions
of political responsibility are becoming aware that the regulatory
capacities of modern welfare states are subject to increasing
restrictions. This does not need to, but can clearly be seen as hav-

ing, a negative impact on interaction between the forces in society in the individual member states of the European Union (EU).

One of the SPD's election pledges in the 2005 *Bundestag* election campaign was, as it says in the manifesto, to 'manage in a humane way' the effects of globalisation. In other words: politicians must seek to analyse the mechanisms of globalisation and find ways to separate the positive effects from the negative ones. In this context, every measure must be examined in terms of its ability to improve people's opportunities in life.

The future of the European Union, too, is closely linked to the question of the extent to which it is able to understand the challenges and opportunities inherent in globalisation and to turn them into practical politics. Gerhard Schröder was right when he warned: 'All too often people regard the regulations of the internal market not as a shield against expanding globalisation, but as quite the opposite: the internal market is viewed as the vanguard, by some even as the Trojan horse, of intensifying competition.' (*Die Zeit*, No. 43/2005)

Neglect of Social Aspects Puts the Whole European Union Project at Risk

An analysis of the social dimension of the European integration process shows that the social question has not played an equal role in practical politics – no matter what may be claimed to the contrary. Whereas the strategy proclaimed at the outset was 'peace through integration', this has since the 1970s/1980s been joined by the 'economic success through integration' slogan. The challenges posed by the disappearance of the blocs at the beginning of the 1990s again reinfor-20

This is demonstrated by the increasing failures of current European policy: the outcome of the referendums on the Constitution in the founding members France and the Netherlands, the failure to reach agreement on finances at the June 2005 summit, the bitter dispute over the 'services directive', or the decidedly low-key start of what had originally been heralded as a promising new orientation of the Lisbon Agenda for growth and employment.

On closer inspection, it becomes clear that the crisis the European Union is widely held to be in is the result not least of the neglect of the social dimension at European level. It is rooted in the citizens' fears of job losses, a fall in prosperity and social exclusion, and their feeling that these fears are not being taken seriously by the acting political elites. The current debates we are having about the European Union are not so much concerned with fundamental issues of political integration, but rather with the sense and impact of European economic integration against the backdrop of globalisation.

Thus the decisive concerns of those who opposed the Constitution were not so much about the Treaty's envisaged changes to the institutional make-up of the European Union or the need for a Common Foreign and Security Policy (CFSP) and for joint solutions, for instance on immigration policy and combating terrorism. Rather, the rejection of the Constitution was overwhelmingly a reflection of the loss of confidence in the mantra-like appeals for liberalisation and promises of prosperity constantly repeated by political leaders. Whereas citizens' latent disaffection with Europe had previously manifested itself most obviously in the ongoing decline in turn-out for elections to the European Parliament, there is now the danger of open resistance to policies made in Brussels and ultimately of the erosion of the entire European project.

In the fierce debates on the 'services directive', the Commission failed to recognise and to develop solutions for the potential undesirable social and ecological repercussions of the liberalisation it favoured on the basis of the country of origin principle. Here, the answer lies neither in the forced opening of the services market nor in the closure of the domestic market to the allegedly cheap Polish plumber supposedly working to lower standards, to use a favourite stereotype of the critics of this directive.

In member states with high unemployment rates, such as Germany and France, attitudes to the new central and eastern European members are shaped by the expectation of increasing pressure on domestic labour markets. The perceived threat to welfare and livelihoods is a further factor.

In addition, there is the never-ending stream of reports about companies relocating to central and eastern Europe despite above-average revenues (e.g. Otis), the breaking-up of well-placed companies by financial investors (e.g. Grohe), waves of redundancies despite high profits (e.g. Deutsche Post) and company closures to remove competitors (e.g. NorskHydro). Against this background, statements about how the increase in market-motivated direct investments by German companies and financial institutions in other member states of the European Union help to secure jobs at home are not really much comfort either.

For many decades the European integration project derived its legitimacy from securing and increasing the prosperity it gave the citizens of its member states. Against the backdrop of globalisation and the resulting increased pressure of competition on the European economies, this source of legitimacy is vanishing. In a European Union in which over 19 million people are without jobs and whose states are demanding welfare and financial cutbacks from their citizens, people rightly expect answers and solutions. In the worst case the European Union is perceived as the vanguard of a globalisation whose sole objective is to enforce pure market economics according to the neo-liberal creed. On the other hand, there is simultaneously the idea that Europe should be a bulwark providing protection against the effects of globalisation. Both views are misleading. For in the best case the European Union will develop into an area in which the advantages of globalisation benefit everyone and the negative aspects are countered with safeguard mechanisms.

Challenges to a Social Democratic European Policy
The challenge to social democratic policy in Europe must therefore be: 'shape globalisation in a social way'. The task of policy-makers is to regulate the creation and distribution of potential profits in order to reach all sections of the population if at all possible. The negative repercussions of globalisation,

such as job insecurity, the increased risk of poverty and the risk of social exclusion, are after all the result not of the process *per se*, but of the lack of an international regulatory framework and the weakening of national regulatory mechanisms. Accordingly, the framework conditions must at last be shaped at national, European and global level. To this end, social democracy must establish itself in the member states and at European level as a force which does not sacrifice social solidarity to a blind race for competitiveness. It must tackle the question of how to protect those people who are among the losers under globalisation, and what must be demanded of these people and how they can be assisted in their individual efforts to adapt. At the same time, it cannot and must not join the ranks of left- and right-wing deniers of reality who propagate protectionism, closed borders and renationalisation as suitable instruments to protect against the negative effects of globalisation.

This does not mean that the social security systems in the member states have to be harmonised. The European Constitutional Treaty rightly denies the European Union the necessary competencies and, given the varying framework conditions and traditions, it would be hard to grant it them. Nevertheless, social democrats must continue to fight for minimum welfare standards in Europe. The 'agency workers' directive' and the 'working time directive' must reflect this.

With regard to the Lisbon strategy, it remains to be seen whether Commission President Barroso will keep his word as regards his vehement denial that the new Lisbon Agenda prioritises competitiveness at the expense of the social dimension. Like Poul Nyrup Rasmussen, we urge that the European social models, aimed at social compensation, be recognised as an advantage of Europe as a business location. The Lisbon strategy certainly does not advocate the end of the welfare state. On the contrary, it calls for it to be modernised as an efficient, proactive state. It must ensure that its citizens have equal access to the best possible education and can participate in lifelong learning. It must actively promote research and development with huge amounts of investment. It must create the environment not only for more jobs, but for better jobs. Concepts such as 'Flexicurity' – which has been successfully implemented in Denmark, and which combines high demands for workers' flexibility and initiative with a high level of social security – may serve as models. Rather than unhelpful promises of full employment, frequently found in the Commission's publications, social democratic policies must find ways to integrate the long-term unemployed with no hope of finding jobs into society, for instance through community employment.

Social democratic policy on Europe must be vigorously committed to bringing about an end to the ruinous tax-cutting competition which has been intensified by the accession of countries such as Slovakia and Estonia with their low flat-tax rates. The harmonisation of the assessment basis for company taxation and the introduction of minimum tax rates must be on the European agenda. If countries with low tax rates also benefit from European structural and regional policy funding, it is an injustice for which there can be no convincing justification and which ultimately will seriously endanger the fragile intra-European solidarity. This approach must also be reflected in the new rules on state aids and on the structural funds. For instance, there should be no possibility of granting assistance to companies which relocate in and outside the European Union or which threaten to do so. Relocations must not be subsidised.

The aim must be to work with trade unions to prevent workers from being played off against each other within the European Union. This is a major challenge for trade unions and for their associations at European level. To date, the Europeanisation of trade unions has not been a great success. Trade unions in the more highly developed economies in particular must at last realise that a purely national viewpoint will in the end weaken them. Specifically, this means that there must be a marked increase in funding on the part of the trade unions. A proactive campaign to establish the social responsibility of policy-makers and the business sector must continue across the European Union. The social dialogue with the European employers' associations, which has been ongoing since 1985 with only rudimentary success so far, could be one of the instruments for this. The enforcement of high standards of employee participation in Europe-wide companies points in the right direction.

Another field requiring action is the international financial markets. The total volume of worldwide transactions is 1.9 trillion US dollars per day of trading. Approximately 3 to 5 per cent of this refers to trade in goods and services. The rest is purely speculative. International agreements must at last be reached on taxing purely speculative financial transfers in the country of origin. The modern banking sector's information and communications systems have long provided the means for this. Further, the European Union can play a pioneering role and create transparency regarding hedge funds and private equity funds. It would be conceivable, for example, to prescribe equity quotas for these funds in order to make it more difficult for them to leverage company takeovers. The European Union, given its responsibility for the free movement of capital, would certainly have the possibility of legislating in this field, for instance with a directive on the control of private equity funds.

At the European level the negotiations on the medium-term EU budget offered a chance to exert pressure. For example, sometime in the foreseeable future at least, all European subsidies need to be reviewed, including the 2002 compromise on the Common Agricultural Policy (CAP). The effect of the cohesion and structural funds must be critically examined. Not because there is a lack of willingness to show solidarity with the structurally weakest regions, but because doubts about the efficiency of redistribution at European level are permissible. The globalisation fund suggested by Barroso suffers not only from fundamental problems with implementation, but also from the fact that its volume – 500 million Euro per year – is much too small to have any relevant economic impact, as well as placing an additional burden on net contributors. The European Union's strength does not lie in the creation of ever more new funds or in the redistribution of ever larger amounts of money. Instead, the Community should take more action in the regulatory sphere, while keeping in mind the social dimension of the Single Market. In light of its existing legislative competencies and the 'open method of coordination' in the field of employment and social policy, it has the necessary instruments at its disposal. What the Commission and the national governments lack, in contrast to the European Parliament, is the political will. Social democratic policy on Europe will have to do much more here in the future.

Europe as an Opportunity
Only a transnational power with the stature of the European Union can influence the contours and course of globalisation. There is no other association of states in the world in which economic integration has been followed by such a high degree of political integration. The unique supranational framework for action and the unparalleled close cooperation among member states in all policy spheres offer ideal conditions for shaping the globalisation process in a social way and gearing it towards social inclusion, as demanded at a global level in the February 2004 report of the International Labour Organisation's (ILO) World Commission on the Social Dimension of Globalisation. Otherwise there is, in the long term, the risk of social unrest even on this most prosperous continent. Recent events in the French suburbs have given us an indication.

Europe must persuade its citizens that it is better equipped to meet the challenges of globalisation than its individual member states. European integration can only be successfully continued if its social dimension is at last filled with life and dynamism. Herein lie both the responsibility of social democratic European policy and its big chance. And herein lies also the chance for the European Union.

Present and Future of the European Union

By Alfred Gusenbauer

In 1945, in the wake of the disasters of fascism and national socialism, it was certainly a wise decision that a group of European states resolved to agree on a common political goal, which consisted in the resolution not to wage war ever again, and to replace this most horrific of wars with peaceful coexistence and cooperation. I emphasise this fact, because I have the impression that, sometimes, the objectives of the European project become blurred, considering that the main goal was to end war and to build peace in Europe. Economic interests and economic cooperation have never been more than instruments in achieving and maintaining peace in Europe. They never were the true objective of the integration process. Actually the approach was much more comprehensive, since the conclusion drawn from the terrible experience of war was to make prosperity as well as the social and personal welfare of the people living on our continent the principle goal. This has, to this day, remained the core objective of European integration, and

I believe that when shaping European policies and European institutions we should keep this core objective in mind.

For quite some time, I had the impression that the European Union had come to understand that the liberalisation of markets and trade alone would not be sufficient to reach the goal of bringing prosperity to as many people in Europe as possible. As a consequence, social and employment policies figured more prominently on the European agenda, especially in the second half of the 1990s, and with Austria as a notable lobbyist. One might say that this change of mind found its most widely known expression in the adoption of the Lisbon goals. However, in the past couple of years, the Lisbon process has got bogged down, and the mid-term review revealed that in many respects we are currently further away from reaching the set objectives than ever before.

As the effective implementation of social and employment policies in Europe was slowing down, or as a consequence thereof, the European Union's political decision-making capacity went into serious crisis, which manifested itself in different areas. There are the well-known frictions over the question of which position to take on the Iraq war; there were widely diverging views in the Constitutional Convention on the future institutional development of Europe; there is disagreement on the deepening of the European Union (EU); and apparently there is no common ground when it comes to defining the policy priorities in setting Europe's medium-term course.

Against this background the rising popularity of political groups whose main interest is the removal of trade barriers and who have little or no interest in the European Union playing a major role in shaping the future of Europe is hardly surprising.

I believe that the development we have witnessed in recent years, which has been marked by restricted political decision-making capacity coupled with the displacement of social and employment policies as well as with a displacement of the specific continental European economic and social model, has been the source of the severe social crisis we are currently facing in

Europe. Luckily this crisis does not manifest itself as explosively throughout Europe as it did during the youth riots in the *banlieus* of Paris in the autumn of 2005. However, it is undisputed that Europe is facing a social crisis. And all those who interpret the events in the suburbs of Paris first and foremost from a security or crime perspective should ask themselves the following question: does anyone believe that these riots would have taken place if all of those young people had jobs?

I believe that anyone asking this question will soon come to the conclusion that at the core of this overall crisis there is a social crisis as well as a crisis of the economy, which offers a growing number of individuals an ever-decreasing range of opportunities and hopes. I therefore believe that a firm commitment to an economic and social model which, in contrast to a radically neo-liberal model, offers a reasonable balance between competition and solidarity, must be put at the top of the social democratic political agenda. This has become a question of survival also for political integration, and we must, therefore, bring about a change in the social and economic conditions in Europe.

Jürgen Habermas was right when he said that governments that pursue interventionist rather than neo-liberal policies can only realise their visions of a prosperous European society if they are able to rely on a healthy European Union, capable of speaking with one voice at the international level. In other words, it will be much easier to resolve the social crisis Europe is currently facing, given the economic conditions prevailing at the international level, if Europe is highly integrated rather than restricted to the present dimensions of the European Single Market. Thus strengthened, Europe would be the response to, rather than the expression of, globalisation. Nowadays many people get the impression that events at large, that is to say globalisation on an international scale, will inevitably hit Europe like acts of God, with one-dimensional consequences, and that current European Union policies provide no answers to globalisation. If we can agree that Europe is not supposed to be an expression of globalisation, but a tentative response to it, the subsequent consensus might be the starting point for a common strategy of social democratic or centre-left parties in Europe.

Incidentally, these ideas are not limited to social democratic thinking. The Christian Democratic Prime Minister of Luxembourg, Jean-Claude Junker, for example, repeatedly stated that workers' interests deserve greater consideration in the European Union, and that Europe is not the Europe of ministers of finance and bankers, the Europe of bureaucrats and foreign ministers. Europe must also be a Europe of the people, people who have a right to feel at home on this continent, because they can enjoy the benefits of a social model that corresponds to their aspirations and views of a good life.

In the given context I consider this the most crucial issue. The European model is unthinkable without a social dimension. Vladimír Špidla, the EU Commissioner for Employment, Social Affairs, and Equal Opportunities, expressed this thought very accurately when he said: 'The European Social Model is based on a set of common values. These values are shared among all member states. Among these fundamental values are the commitment to democracy, the rejection of all forms of discrimination, universal access to education, accessible and good quality health care, gender equality, solidarity and equity, the recognition of the role of the social partners, and of social dialogue. These values are constitutive for Europe. In other words, Europe ends where these values are not shared.' To my mind, this is an excellent description of the constitutive character of the social dimension for both European identity and the European civilisation model. Consequently, the purpose of European integration is to remove frictions, not only as regards interstate conflicts, which in the past gave rise to wars, but also when it comes to remedying the gap between rich and poor, between those who are accepted and respected in their communities, and those who are excluded, between those who have a share in economic progress and those who do not.

I am of the opinion that the admission of the central and eastern European countries to the European Union has taken us a big stride forward towards this goal, since the historical interstate demarcation lines have been overcome. However, this does not relieve us from the task of working on the implementation of policies designed to overcome the demarcation lines dividing the societies of today. Still, we need to ask ourselves whether, subsequent to this historic enlargement by the central and eastern European countries, continued high-speed enlargement may not impair the European Union's decision-making capacity when it comes to intrastate conflicts. To put it frankly, I am less concerned about potential member states fulfilling the admission criteria, than about the absorption capacity of the Union itself. Currently we experience how, even under the prevailing conditions, it is extremely difficult to reach agreement on the funding of EU policies, and how the principle of solidarity – a fundamental principle of Community action – is quite obviously twisted and abused by individual member states in a highly selfish manner. Solidarity depends on reciprocity; it applies to everyone, also to the new member states, and does not permit any kind of discounts. Nor can I personally understand how it can be justified that new member states benefiting from the principle of solidarity and availing themselves of European funds, just like older member states that face structural difficulties, use these benefits to finance tax and in particular profit tax dumping, which puts the overall financing of the European welfare state at risk.

I believe that the prevailing conditions call for a fundamental re-definition of the concept of solidarity, which needs to be made fairer. To maintain currently claimed and exercised entitlements holds the danger that new challenges will not be addressed, that special interests are shored up and that the integration project will fall victim to them.

Even before the failure of the referendums in France and the Netherlands, I felt that the European Union was in trouble. Signs of crisis had been noticeable for quite some time. Europe needs to enter into a dialogue with its citizens, especially on one key issue: how can the population tangibly benefit from European integration in their daily lives? Personally, I believe that the people of Europe cannot be blamed for being dissatisfied with current results of European political decision-making. In the light of weak growth rates, persistently high unemployment and the growing gap between rich and poor, they cannot be blamed for questioning the purpose served by Europe. While it is our obligation to highlight the European Union's role in maintaining peace, I feel that this argument alone is no longer sufficient in ascertaining people's loyalty to the European project.

This is why I would consider it perfectly reasonable and about time to address this dissatisfaction with the present state of Europe, which is being articulated by citizens all around Europe. Such a confrontation with people's concerns will inevitably lead to the question of what should be the nature of policy change in Europe. What needs to be done differently in order to increase the practical benefits people can draw from Union membership?

I believe that practical benefits will increase once we succeed in effectively combating unemployment in Europe, which might be achieved to a limited extent at the national level, but would certainly be more successful if agreed at the international level. If Austria decided today to implement an expansive economic policy, the situation would be improved, though some of the positive effects would evaporate unless Austria's neighbouring countries, or the countries in the Eurozone, adopted a similar or the same economic policy. This implies that, apart from the many tasks to be performed at the national level, effectively combating unemployment is a key task of the European Union if the European project is to be taken forward in the best interest of Europe's citizens.

Another thing: one may disagree with some of Tony Blair's policies; however, I agree with him when he says that traditional agricultural subsidies which first and foremost benefit large agricultural enterprises, rather than small and organic farmers, are too high and that a Europe which looks to the future and intends to present a response to globalisation must be a Europe that invests much more into science, research and universities. He concludes that the European Union's traditional agricultural subsidies must decrease in favour of increased spending on science and research. I believe that this approach is much better suited to meet the challenges currently faced by Europe than the preservation of vested interests.

Tony Blair is right when he says: 'If we want our economy to meet the future challenges, at some point we have got to make sure that the budget is aligned with the economic priorities of our citizens, of our businesses and of our workforce.'

Consequently it would have been necessary to realign Europe's political priorities also in the context of the negotiations on the Community budget. It is a pity that these negotiations ended in a lukewarm compromise, with policy and expenditure structures being preserved up to the year 2013. The vague declaration of intent to evaluate the budget development again in 2008 does not really help. In fact, the same misguided budgetary policy has been prolonged until the year 2013. This will perpetuate the excessive funding of agricultural structures, which, *inter alia*, causes large swathes of land in Europe to become wasteland and ruins farmers in developing countries, thus running counter to any kind of solidarity-based development approach. I think it would have been wiser to go on negotiating and haggling than to perpetuate misguided policies for years to come. No extra money for research and development until the year 2013 clearly disadvantages a Europe that competes for knowledge, competes for the best brains and competes in the development of goods and services that prove successful on the world market. I believe that Europe needs to set new priorities, focusing on research and development, on promoting growth and infrastructure, better coordination of tax policies, and – a particularly pressing issue – on aligning migration policies.

Hans Rauscher, a renowned Austrian columnist, very accurately analysed the dilemma we are facing today: a cheap, low-skilled workforce is being lured from different parts of the world to perform hard, dirty and dangerous jobs for little pay – Rauscher calls this type of work 'donkeywork'. Meanwhile, however, there is not enough of this type of work available.

As a result, the young, mostly second-generation immigrants, are out of 'donkeywork', for which their parents had been originally hired, and as a result suffer from a particular type of disorientation and hopelessness.

There is only one possible response to this situation, namely to invest enormous amounts into establishing an educational system that provides equal opportunities for all students. The member states at the centre of Europe, most notably Austria and Germany, need to point the finger of blame at themselves, since their educational systems are designed to perpetuate ethnic and social differences. An educational system that serves integration and overcomes differences of ethnic and social origin will be much better suited to provide life chances to migrants and their children. To reform our educational systems to this effect seems to be a key task when it comes to tackling the existing challenges.

Europe is having a hard time because its mechanisms of legitimisation are immensely complex. What am I trying to say? Nobody dissatisfied with Austrian domestic policies will immediately question the legitimacy of the Austrian nation, but rather come to the more logical conclusion that the malperforming administration will have to be replaced at the next elections. It is different with Europe. If people are, for various reasons, dissatisfied with European policies, they tend to question the European Union's very right of existence, for the simple reason that its mechanism of legitimisation is different. There is no such thing as an ingrained European identity. Europe needs to justify its right of existence ever anew, through political decision-making and performance. The European Union is thus exposed to much higher pressure to perform than its member states. The absence of adequate mechanisms for getting rid of unloved politicians adds to the problem. In a nation state it is easy. There are elections to the national parliament and the unpopular government is voted out of power and replaced with another one, which is given the opportunity to prove its superiority. But how to vote someone out of power at European level, considering the complex system of institutions – Parliament, Council, Commission – and the fact that most citizens have no idea what their decision-making powers are? As an ordinary citizen I simply do not have the power to vote those responsible out of office. Such power, however, is a fundamental precondition of democracy: it is the requirement that those subjected to standards, i.e. the citizens, may choose to rid themselves of their rulers. This is the difference between democracies and non-democratic systems of government. Of course there are other differences, but the core difference is: how do I get rid of my rulers? At the European Union level people see no way of voting those whose policies they disapprove of out of power, not even with a differently composed European Parliament, which would naturally make a difference.

This is why I have for quite some time been of the opinion that, if we wish to strengthen Europe, we must have direct elections of the agents of government. One option would be for the President of the EU Commission to be determined by the result of the elections to the European Parliament. Another option would be the direct election of a European President, even if it does not correspond to the constitutional tradition of the majority of member states. So, there are various options, but to my mind we must inevitably move in this direction if we wish to make the interplay between government and opposition, between satisfaction and dissatisfaction, visible to European citizens. I think this would be important and therefore regret that the Draft Constitution has, so far, failed to be adopted, as it would bring considerable improvement, especially in the given context. Also, as regards the rights of the European Parliament, the Constitution would mark considerable progress. There is a danger that in the event of the European Constitution not being adopted, any further democratisation of the Union will be seriously delayed, adding to the above discussed problem rather than rectifying it.

It must also be pointed out that political parties, as major actors in democratic systems at least at national level, have to this day failed to establish proper European structures comparable to the structures at national level. I am not excluding the European social democratic parties from this criticism. We still have more of an association or federation of different national parties than a real European social democratic party, and the same is true for other political groups.

I do believe that without establishing political parties at the European level there will never be sufficient public awareness in and of Europe, and there will never be that badly needed European political space without which the above-outlined objectives of integration cannot be reached.

So we find ourselves in a paradoxical situation. On the one hand, the citizens of Europe have high expectations of Europe; on the other hand, there is little willingness to provide the European Union with the tools it needs to achieve these goals. Frequently, petty interest-driven disputes arise, which are not only harmful to European creativity, European visions and the 'European Dream', but what is much worse, are in many instances harmful to the best interests of the European population. In the absence of a consensus on a great vision for Europe, I am in favour of doing what is feasible and serves the prosperity and wellbeing of the European people. I agree with Timothy Garton Ash, a truly eminent expert on European affairs, who wrote in *The Guardian* at the end of October 2005: 'Europe should be like a great experimental laboratory, with countries constantly looking over each other's shoulders and stealing each other's best ideas... We agree on the goals: higher growth and productivity, more innovation, less unemployment, reduced poverty. We don't all need to get there by the same route.' This is a pragmatic approach to tackling some of the most pressing social and economic issues in Europe, and thereby regaining sufficient momentum, so that people do not think of Europe in sceptical terms only, and that our vision of deeper integration may be eventually realised.

A Democratic Left Vision for Europe

By David Clark, Neil Kinnock, Michael Leahy,
Ken Livingstone, John Monks and Stephen Twigg

Preface

In a very direct sense this statement is part of Robin Cook's
political legacy. He suggested it at a meeting of leading Labour
pro-Europeans that took place in the Gay Hussar restaurant in
Soho the evening after the French referendum rejecting the
European Constitutional Treaty. The meeting had been organised to plan a British referendum campaign, but became instead
a postmortem on the defeat. True to his character, Robin was
determined that pro-Europeans should not wallow in despair,
but should regroup and set out some practical steps as part of a
new and more effective campaign to make the case for Europe.
He conceived this statement as the first of those steps. Sadly, it
turned out to be the last project I worked with him on after more
than a decade of political collaboration.

The statement itself reflects the views of its signatories, but
Robin's presence can still be felt. He had seen and approved an

early draft and an extended discussion about it had been the subject of our last meeting a few days before his death. He was so absorbed by the subject that he asked for a revised version to be emailed to a hotel in the Highlands where he was due to be staying on 7th August 2005. He never got there. I have no doubt that had Robin lived to see the final draft he would have gone through it and added his own hand-written amendments as I had seen him do on countless occasions before. But the thrust of its argument – that the democratic left should embrace the European Union as a vehicle for progressive change – was very much his own. It can be seen as an authentic statement of his political beliefs.

The origins of Robin's emergence as a leading pro-European have been the subject of extensive commentary, much of it ill-informed. One particularly erroneous theory is that he 'went native' under the influence of officials at the Foreign Office. This conveniently ignores the fact that he had become convinced of the case for European integration long before Labour took office in 1997. He was, as he often pointed out, the Shadow Europe Minister appointed by Neil Kinnock to move Labour away from a position of withdrawal after the 1983 election defeat.

The evolution of Robin's thinking on Europe was gradual. He voted for withdrawal in 1975 when Europe was seen as little more than a common market, but later started to reassess his position when Europe's potential as a political and social project started to become more apparent. By the 1990s he had come to the view that globalisation had limited the ability of nation states to address the most serious challenges on their own, and that the future of progressive politics lay in deeper international cooperation and European integration in particular. It was a conclusion that fitted naturally with his internationalist instincts. Britain, he believed, would never succeed in the wider world unless it was first able to make common cause with its nearest neighbours.

He remained critical of specific aspects of European Union (EU) politics. The last time I saw him he was complaining about what he saw as the European Commission's unwarranted interference in the British horse racing industry, something that was even closer to his heart than Europe. But he remained convinced that Britain, and the labour movement in particular, should see the European Union as an opportunity, not a threat, and was dismissive of the idea that Britain could opt out.

To the surprise of many, Robin thrived on the European stage during his time as Foreign Secretary. Those who knew him mainly through his combative performances at the despatch box in the House of Commons would have struggled to recognise the Robin Cook who worked the corridors of Brussels, patiently building consensus and agreement. By the end of his time as Foreign Secretary, his officials believed he had become the most respected and influential foreign minister in Europe. But Robin was not just a great diplomat for his country. His vision of Europe was deeply political and his work reflected a profound commitment to the solidarity of nations and peoples. One of his proudest achievements was to have served as President of the Party of European Socialists from 2001 until 2004.

Robin disdained the individualist school of history and would have been angered by the suggestion that the European cause had been weakened in any fundamental way by his passing. But the truth remains that those in the labour movement who support Britain's full engagement in Europe have lost a true friend and an inspirational leader. Those he leaves behind owe it to his memory to continue the fight in his absence.
David Clark

A Democratic Left Vision for Europe
We are at a decisive moment in the development of both the European Union and the democratic Left. Indeed, it is our contention that the prospects of both are closely linked. The European Left cannot realise its vision of a more just social order on a continent that is economically and politically fragmented. Europe cannot succeed unless it responds effectively to the demands of ordinary Europeans for material security and social justice. To doubt either of these fundamental truths would be a

costly error. It is for this reason that we call on pro-Europeans in the labour movement to unite and challenge those who see in Europe's present difficulties an opportunity to weaken it or push it in a more neo-liberal direction.

The insight that the peoples of the world are united by common interests and a common humanity is obviously not a recent product of the global era; it has been central to the socialist idea since its birth. Yet the democratic Left has often failed to translate its internationalist values into the practical reality of a progressive world order built on strong and effective institutions. The European Union is certainly not perfect, but it is the most advanced and successful international organisation that has ever been created. For all its faults, it is living proof of humanity's capacity to set aside deep national differences and order its affairs in common. That is too precious an achievement to be squandered lightly or ever jeopardised by neglect.

The democratic Left case for modernising reform of the European Union is certainly strong, but no one should harbour any illusions that there is an accessible alternative path to the sort of world we want. The collapse of the European project would not herald a new era of progressive advance: it would condemn Europe to the economic and political rivalry that has proved so ruinous in the past. It is therefore the responsibility of the labour movement and its allies across Europe, to build on what has already been achieved and make the case for radical change from within.

The corollary of this is that Europe must be more than a marketplace for the free movement of goods, services, labour and capital. It must be an instrument for regulating markets in the public interest and restoring human values to the economic life of our continent and the wider world. This is Europe's rationale and its real achievement: not simply the promotion of free-trade, but the creation of a framework that allows trade to be managed in accordance with rules and institutions that are politically determined by elected governments. In the real world this is something that even the largest European countries can no longer hope to achieve on their own and must now do by acting collectively. Real progress has already been made on consumer standards, environmental protection, social rights and much else. But Europe has the potential and the need to do a great deal more simply because the greatest challenges, opportunities and threats it faces today are transnational in scope.

The purpose of this statement is therefore twofold: to restate the democratic Left case for the political and economic integration of Europe and to set out a vision of how the European Union could be reformed to make it a more effective instrument for social and economic progress. No one imagines that this will be easy, but the alternative of disillusionment followed by disintegration would be a catastrophe for progressive politics and the security of nations.

The European Crisis
The failure of the European Constitutional Treaty to win popular approval in the French and Dutch referendums is a symptom, not the cause, of a crisis in European politics. Support for the European Union has declined sharply in the last decade and a half: down from 72 per cent across all member states in 1990 to 54 per cent today. In the same period, support in Britain has slumped from 57 per cent to 36 per cent. Yet most of Europe's political elites have failed to heed the warning signs. European decision-making has remained too technocratic and remote, too focused on process over outcome and insufficiently interested in meeting the challenges of public perception, understanding and consent.

Very few Europeans see the European Union as essential to their well-being. Indeed, few have a particularly clear idea of what it is for. Some of that can be attributed to the passage of time and events over the last fifty years. But the deeper reality is that without a clear reason for existence, the European Union will increasingly be seen as just another layer of bureaucracy, or worse, part of a wider phenomenon in which people feel themselves to be at the mercy of anonymous global processes beyond their control. This prevailing uncertainty and insecurity is exploited by nationalist and populist movements, who advocate a retreat into old certainties, largely imagined, and practise the politics of national and ethnic exclusion. Unless Europe comes to be seen as part of the solution to the day-to-day challenges of life and work, it will always be seen as a problem.

The mixture of public puzzlement and suspicion about the European Union translates into a perceived lack of 'legitimacy'. That is substantially the result of failures of political courage, vision and consistent advocacy. Europe's leaders have not taken responsibility for explaining the benefits and potential of integration to citizens and have too often found it convenient to blame 'Brussels' when things go wrong. They have also failed to construct a political vision in which a more integrated Europe with relevant policies and accountable institutions is seen to play an essential role in enlarging the sovereignty and safeguarding the interests of each member state. This is part of a broader trend of declining faith in the ability of government to change people's lives for the better, but it is something which successive governments in several member states have fuelled themselves.

In this respect the European crisis is a particular problem for the Left. Those who are happy for the fate of humanity to be determined by the invisible hand of market forces or the aggregate of private choices believe they have nothing to fear from a world in which politics remains purely national. Indeed, they prefer conditions in which the decisions that matter are beyond the sovereign reach of elected governments. By contrast, for those who believe that people should be able to shape their own future, consciously and through their elected representatives, the need for a strong, effective and relevant European Union with accountable institutions should be clear.

Yet in Britain, the pro-European consensus that formed part of Labour's revival in the late 1980s and early 1990s has come under strain. As in France and other countries, parts of the mainstream Left say that they are disillusioned with the apparent retreat from the social vision of Europe outlined by Jacques Delors in his speech to the Trades Union Congress (TUC) in 1988 and emphasised by those who changed Labour's policy direction in those years. There has been a reaction against what sometimes seems to be a one-sided emphasis on market liberalisation that has expressed itself in a growing scepticism about the value and purpose of European integration.

The Labour government bears a measure of responsibility for this apparent weakening of the pro-European coalition. After initially taking a strong and practical pro-European stance, it has dissipated scarce political capital in seeming to appease elements of the Right – particularly in the media – that will never be reconciled to the European Union. That deficiency is being paid for with a loss of support on the Left. It makes no sense for Labour ministers to return from major treaty negotiations declaring that their main achievement was to ensure that the treaty would do nothing to improve employment and social rights. That is not an approach that is likely to unite or inspire the labour movement or anyone else who wants economic change to be accompanied by social progress.

In his warmly received speech to the European Parliament, Tony Blair said that he wanted a political and 'Social Europe', not just a free-trade zone. That is a sentiment everyone in the labour movement and the wider European Left must heartily applaud. But words are no substitute for action and the positions taken by the British Labour government on, for instance, working time and information and consultation rights for employees have too often appeared to conflict with that aspiration. It is time for greater consistency of purpose and political action. The task for the pro-European Left must be to contribute to that goal by developing and articulating a clear agenda for the reform and renewal of the European project in a progressive direction.

Europe: a Union of Values
For all its present problems, European integration is a phenomenal success story. It has achieved the original purpose of the

Community of making war between its members unthinkable, so much so that the peace of Europe is generally taken for granted. It has constructed the largest and richest single market in the world, boosting jobs, growth and living standards. It has given millions of EU citizens the opportunity to travel from their home country to live and work in other parts of the Union. It is the largest trading bloc on the planet with the potential to use that power to address global imbalances while building its own future prosperity. It has shown solidarity with Europe's poorer regions by providing structural funding and helping countries like Ireland and Spain to make huge advances towards prosperity. It has become the biggest provider of humanitarian aid and untied development assistance in the world. It has promoted political change by embracing new democracies in central and eastern Europe and facilitating their reform and reconstruction.

In the last decade, the European Union has undertaken its two most ambitious projects to date: the creation of a single currency embracing twelve states and successive rounds of enlargement that have more than doubled its membership from twelve to twenty-five. Change is always disruptive and it was perhaps inevitable that undertaking both projects simultaneously would provoke a negative reaction in some sections of public opinion. But the fact that Europe has successfully completed them ought to be enough to dispel the fashionable thesis that European integration is in decline.

The list of countries queuing to join the European Union and aspiring to be part of the Eurozone continues to grow and around the world regional formations like Mercosur, the African Union and the Association of South-East Asian Nations (ASEAN) are now attempting to emulate Europe's achievements. The current mood of Euro-pessimism is fundamentally at odds with the reality of Europe's strength and future potential. Our political leaders should acknowledge that fact and make the argument for Europe with greater clarity and confidence. If they do not, secessionists – mainly on the Right – will benefit. Diffidence about Europe does not just mean criticism from pro-Europeans. It means votes for parties that sow and harvest isolationist sentiments.

It is clear, of course, that public support for Europe cannot and should not be secured or retained simply by dwelling on past successes. That support can only be won if Europe continues to adapt, move forward and provide practical solutions to modern problems. The vision of a peaceful and united continent built gradually on foundations of economic cooperation made sense in the ruins of a war-ravaged Europe. But the objectives of putting an end to war on our continent and creating an economic community are no longer sufficient to sustain the process of integration. The first is too remote from the experience or perspective of most modern Europeans, the second too managerial and depoliticised.

If it is to thrive in the twenty-first century, European integration needs a renewed sense of purpose, one that is capable of commanding the understanding and support of the peoples of Europe and not just its political elites. It is our conviction that the foundations of the European project should be its common values, a shared commitment to put them into practice and a belief that they offer the best route to security and prosperity.

Europe's values are clearly demonstrated in many comparative surveys of international opinion. European nations represent a diverse spectrum of experiences and ideas, yet they have in common a clearly identifiable set of political and social perceptions and preferences, which are the product of the continent's unique history and culture. These are clearly evident across a broad range of economic, social, international and moral issues. The Pew Global Attitudes Surveys provide just one of the authoritative sources for this conclusion.

Asked whether it is more important for government to guarantee that no one should be in need or for people to be free from government, Europeans chose the former by margins of approximately two to one: Britain 62 per cent – 33 per cent, France 62 per cent – 36 per cent, Germany 57 per cent – 39 per cent and Poland 64 per cent – 31 per cent. Americans, however, chose freedom from government by a margin of 58 per cent to 34 per cent. Those agreeing strongly with the proposition that government has a responsibility to look after the poor were as follows: Britain 59 per cent, France 50 per cent, Germany 45 per cent and Poland 59 per cent. In America just 29 per cent agreed.

This divergence of attitude is not only clear from other similar surveys over many years, it is apparent in the very different policy choices Europeans and Americans make. Whereas European societies exhibit a strong attachment to the welfare state and mechanisms of collective social protection, Americans tend towards a preference for what they see as minimal government and individual responsibility. The reasons for this largely relate to differences of historical experience. Whereas Americans believe that they have created a new world in which the stigma of class status has been removed and individual potential liberated, Europeans still hold that systemic differences in social conditions have a serious and detrimental impact on life chances. Historically, this outlook was represented in the rise of organised labour and democratic socialist ideas and movements, but it also has strong roots in religious social doctrine, which is why the European Social Model continues to enjoy strong support across the political spectrum from left to centre-right.

Similar differences are observable on other issues. Europeans are much more committed than Americans to multilateralism based on international laws and institutions. The belief that United Nations (UN) approval should be secured before the use of military forces runs at 64 per cent in Britain, 63 per cent in France, 80 per cent in Germany and only 41 per cent in America. The nations of Europe are also more secular and socially liberal. 58 per cent of Americans believe that it is necessary to believe in God to be moral compared to only 25 per cent in Britain, 13 per cent in France, 33 per cent in Germany and 38 per cent in Poland.

Plainly, there is nothing anti-American about recognising that Europe is different in cultural and social perceptions and aspirations. Nor should this diminish our desire for a strong and enduring transatlantic partnership. Despite differences of outlook, Europe and America share a common democratic heritage and a joint interest in defending it. But America has never lacked confidence in celebrating its own exceptional identity and nor should Europe. An alliance of equals in which both sides remain true to themselves is more likely to make a positive contribution to the world than one based on apparent domination, with consequent resentment from one direction and arrogance from the other.

It should be clear from this that Europe's common values correspond strongly with those that have defined the labour movement since its inception – internationalism, solidarity, equality and the belief that economic life should be compatible with the needs of society. Labour needs partners in order to realise its political goals and there is nowhere in the world it is more likely to find them than in Europe. It should view any proposal that strengthens Europe's capacity to apply its values in the form of common policies and practical achievements with enthusiasm.

This is particularly important since the evidence shows that those values have broad appeal to the British people. Neither surveys nor experience substantiate the widely proclaimed belief that there is an Old Europe/New Europe divide or the argument that British values are closer to those of America. The populations of the new and old member states think very much alike on the key issues. Indeed, British opinion often emerges as more egalitarian and socially progressive than several other European countries. The belief that there are strong divergences of core values in Europe is an illusion, fostered by the Right, which needs to be robustly challenged with the facts.

Greater consciousness of Europe's shared values is a vital component of any effort to build support for the idea that Europe has a joint interest in combining to promote and defend them. It is also basic to the task of dismantling the prejudices about other Europeans that have been assiduously encouraged by Europhobic forces, particularly those in the British press and parts of British politics. This is a challenge of political leadership in Britain and Europe more widely. It is one Labour must now rise to.

Europe and Globalisation

Clearly, European integration was not conceived as a response to globalisation. When the European Coal and Steel Community was founded in 1951, exchange rates were fixed, environmental problems were regarded as national in scope, international travel and communications were the preserve of elites and states retained a virtual monopoly of armed force. The modern challenges of volatile global markets, climate change, mass migration and international crime and terrorism could not have been foreseen. Yet, by constructing a transnational political space, the countries of Europe have created a framework within which effective responses and solutions to these problems have become possible and, in several spheres, have already been developed. This should be a prime mission for the European Union in the twenty-first century.

To argue that globalisation is either good or bad is simplistic. Its social and economic impact has been too uneven for that sort of judgement to be possible. On the one hand, globalisation makes it possible for many people to have access to the best of what the world has to offer and has the potential to enrich the human experience. On the other, it has created new forms of insecurity and social disruption that need to be remedied. The answer lies not in either isolationism or crude laissez-faire, but in striking the right balance between openness and regulation in the common interest. That is something that can only be achieved through collective action and agreement at an international level.

Too many on the Left accept this analysis without following it through to its logical conclusion. The effective management of global affairs is a huge task and can only be achieved by rules-based international bodies with a strong regulatory capacity. If the European Union, with the strongest set of common institutions and values of any international organisation, is not to form an essential component of this project, then how else is it to be achieved? The Left's internationalism cannot be merely declaratory; it must take a practical form. To imagine that there is a better option on offer is, as Altiero Spinelli once put it, to 'quit the ground of reality to take refuge in vain and cloudy hopes.'

The fact that the peoples of Europe want it to play that role was clear enough in the position taken by many French and Dutch voters in their referendums. Most were not voting to reject European integration as such. They were using the opportunity to call on Europe's leaders to take seriously their desire for greater security and certainty in a rapidly changing world. The response of our leaders cannot simply be to repeat the mantra that 'globalisation is good for you' and that Europe must 'modernise or die' or to appease populist forces that campaigned for 'No' votes with isolationist and racist arguments. If it is, the result will be a rise in support for political movements preaching nationalism, chauvinism and protectionism.

The neo-liberal vision of globalisation as an irresistible force of nature beyond the control of governments is fundamentally at odds with reality. Political power plays a critical role in determining its course. It is striking that the nations that have benefited most from globalisation have done so by ignoring key tenets of neo-liberal ideology. America, China and India are continental-sized nation states with sufficient clout and geopolitical presence to interact with the outside world on their own terms. America uses the international reserve status of the dollar to run external deficits that would force any other country to deflate their economy. The economic modernisation of China, patently not a democracy, has involved a heavy element of state direction in the form of capital controls, along with the state ownership of banks and significant parts of its industry. India, the world's largest democracy, also has capital controls and an interventionist economic policy.

Those penalised by the process of globalisation have been countries with relatively small domestic markets and a correspondingly high dependency on international trade and investment. The financial crises experienced in East Asia and South America, and the persistent underdevelopment and indebtedness of sub-Saharan Africa, are the most obvious examples of how the vulnerable can be affected. But Britain's 1976 International Monetary Fund (IMF) crisis and the capital flight that destabilised the Mitterrand government in France in the early 1980s demonstrate that Europe is not immune to this threat. For the nations of Europe the lesson ought to be self-evident. In globalised conditions – now permanent – they can only hope to safeguard their interests effectively by acting together.

The European Union's goal should be to influence and manage the process of globalisation in ways that maximise its benefits and minimise its costs to Europeans and the wider world. It should seek to emphasise the primacy of democratic politics and ensure that it is used to make the operation of the market compatible with the needs of human society. Central to this must be the creation of a new international economic order in which the pursuit of national advantage dressed up as liberalisation is replaced by a conscious attempt to manage the global economy equitably and in the common interest.

This could have a number of components. One option that deserves positive consideration is a new international system of managed exchange rates and capital controls to prevent speculative financial flows from disrupting otherwise stable economies. In the last decade alone Russia, East Asia and South America have all experienced the chaos and social destruction caused by large and sudden exchange rate movements. But the potential for a much larger crisis is inherent in the huge imbalances that characterise the modern global economy. America's $500bn current account deficit and its dependency on the willingness of East Asian central banks to buy and hold dollars pose a particular problem. A sudden unravelling could create a world recession. The single currency makes Europe a real force in the global economy. That influence should be used to press for a more stable and equitable international monetary order.

A counterpart to this could be a mechanism for managing global trade imbalances. A proposal to achieve this has been put forward by the Fabian Globalisation Group in the form of an international clearing union similar to the one advocated by John Maynard Keynes in the 1940s. The essence of this idea is that countries with trade surpluses would be obliged to recycle them in ways that sustain global economic demand and allow countries with trade deficits to restore balance. Such a system would facilitate free-trade, but in ways that benefit all.

Another objective should be the global benchmarking of social and environmental standards and their integration into the body of world trade rules. There is nothing protectionist about insisting that free-trade should be fair trade. It cannot be acceptable for countries to seek competitive advantage by exploiting their workforce and degrading our common environment. In order to secure guaranteed access to world markets, countries should be expected to meet certain minimum standards. These should be set at realistic levels, but the ambition should be to raise them over time as the living standards of poorer nations begin to rise.

Of course, fairness must cut both ways. European Union countries are not the only ones guilty of disadvantaging the developing world by handing out market distorting agricultural subsidies: America, for instance, protects its farmers with billions of dollars of aid every year. But the European Union should lead the way in abolishing these and other unfair trade practices. Initial steps should include further and more radical reform of the Common Agricultural Policy (CAP), the phased abolition of the sugar regime, the termination of subsidies for agricultural exports and a more substantial opening of European markets to the primary produce of many developing countries.

Finally, there is wider recognition than ever before that it makes material as well as moral sense for management of the global economy to be based on solidarity. Consistent with that, there should be mechanisms of redistribution that replicate the European Union's social and regional policies on a global scale. The development agenda has recently taken a significant forward stride, and Tony Blair and Gordon Brown deserve great credit for the leading role they have played. But there are still doubts about whether the resources and the political will are likely to be evident elsewhere on the scale necessary to meet the UN's Millennium Development Goals. The objective should be to develop a funding stream that is independent of charity and the vagaries of intergovernmental horse-trading. One idea that deserves positive consideration is the French proposal for a levy on international air travel.

These policies would form the basis for a global New Deal: a social and economic compact between the developed and developing worlds in which the rules of globalisation are structured to benefit all. But they presuppose a Europe that is able to speak and act as one. The alternative is a Europe in which there is a multiplicity of national policies with the result that global markets and big and powerful countries shape globalisation to their advantage.

A Sustainable Economic and Social Model

European values are embodied in the political choices Europeans make. In social and economic policy, these include support for political pluralism and democracy, endorsement of the mixed economy and a strong commitment to public welfare, social cohesion and wealth redistribution. It may be something of an over-generalisation to talk about a European Social Model, but there is certainly a common social ideal that is clearly represented in the way European countries seek to guarantee social well-being through collectively funded services, universal entitlements, equitable opportunities for education and employment, and rights to health and safety in life and in work. In Britain, this comes across most obviously in unwavering public support for the National Health Service (NHS) and other features of the welfare state such as free schooling and benefits to the infirm and the elderly.

This social ideal is under ideological attack as never before. Weak growth and stubbornly high levels of unemployment in some of the larger European economies are cited by supporters of the American business model as proof that the social market economy is sclerotic and inefficient. Yet on any objective analysis there is no correlation between levels of labour market regulation, taxation and public spending on the one hand, and economic performance on the other. If there were, the Danish, Swedish, Finnish, Dutch and Austrian economies would be amongst the least successful economies instead of being amongst the best performing.

Indeed, there are good reasons for supposing that these countries have succeeded precisely because they have maintained decent welfare and labour standards and modernised structures to anticipate and match changing economic realities. Because of their small size and greater relative exposure to world trade, these economies have developed programmes of public assistance and strong frameworks of social bargaining that involve trade unions as ways of managing economic change. Since the future of Europe's larger economies is one in which they too will become more integrated into the global economy, there are obvious conclusions to be drawn. There is a proven and practical alternative to neo-liberalism.

Economic reform is certainly needed in Europe, but it should start from a recognition that where countries have been willing to reduce non-wage labour costs, embrace social partnership and adopt welfare systems that train for adaptability and incentivise work, the European Social Model has shown that it is still capable of combining well-developed mechanisms of social protection with improvements in productivity and high and sustained levels of growth and employment. The Lisbon Agenda adopted by the European Union remains the right way forward, but more efforts are needed to raise the proportion of Europeans who are economically active, boost investment in research and development and human capital, promote skills and lifelong learning, and combat social exclusion.

The British Labour government can certainly be proud of its record in creating jobs, expanding the economy, reducing poverty and improving public services. But it should be more ready to acknowledge the extent to which these achievements have been intelligently evolved in other European countries, not least in relation to welfare reforms and active labour market policies. Neither Britain under Labour, nor any other country, has a monopoly of wisdom about how to succeed in the modern world. The need, therefore, is to spread the use of best practice in the delivery of economic efficiency and social justice.

Unfortunately, by being reluctant to acknowledge the European character of many of its most popular and effective policies, the Labour government has allowed itself to become seen, at home and on the continent, as the odd one out. The government's positioning on issues such as the 'working time directive' has created the false impression that Britain's approach is at variance with those of the rest of Europe and helped to obscure its positive achievements, such as the high levels of occupational health and safety performance in the United Kingdom (UK). The effect has been to weaken Britain's influence in Europe and encourage notions of cultural separateness that strengthen anti-European sentiment at home.

Portraying Europe as an economic failure is not only factually inaccurate, it undermines support for integration and fails to provide a realistic assessment of where we stand in relation to our nearest neighbours. Many of our European neighbours have bigger and stronger manufacturing sectors, trade surpluses in comparison to our trade deficit, lower personal debt and higher productivity. Moreover, many still have better public services at the point of use and most experience significantly lower levels of social inequality. In the interests of learning, we should perhaps approach the European debate with more curiosity and less presumption of superiority.

European politics must not be allowed to become a competitive struggle between different national approaches. The basic European Social Model of the future must reflect a synthesis of what is best in each whilst still facilitating advances which accord with national preferences and conditions. In this process, Britain has much to offer, but it also still has much to learn.

Many of these questions are matters of national policy, but Europe has provided an essential framework for economic and social progress by constructing a single market with minimum social standards. There is a compelling case for it to do more, especially in meeting some of the key challenges identified by the Lisbon Agenda, such as social exclusion, the need for higher rates of economic participation, and an ageing society. In view of their importance in influencing economic opportunity and quality of life, particular priority should be given to pre-school education.

There is now clear evidence that the provision of good quality universal childcare and education for the under-fives helps to boost educational performance and promote social mobility. And because it enables many more mothers to seek and gain paid employment, it also helps to raise levels of economic participation, boost growth, advance gender equality, reduce child poverty and increase the birth rate. All of these elements illustrate the way in which social justice and economic efficiency go hand in hand.

A number of European countries already provide universal childcare, and Britain is making strides in that direction, but coverage elsewhere is patchy. The European Union should set minimum standards covering all member states. Those that already provide a service that meets those standards would receive a rebate on their budget contributions. For the rest, the European Union would allocate direct funding to local providers from the voluntary sector. This would obviously require substantial additional resources and part of this could be found from reductions in agricultural spending, but Europe's leaders will need to look again at the overall question of the European Union's budget to find the money needed. The benefits that would accrue from a European childcare guarantee have already been identified as a common interest. Finding those resources is therefore a test of Europe's political will and economic intelligence.

It is clear that the strength of Europe's Social Model will depend ultimately on its economic performance, and coordinated efforts to boost and sustain growth and employment rates must be given fresh impetus. However, Europe will not achieve economic success by deregulating its labour markets and triggering a race to the bottom in employment standards. Supply-side reforms of the right kind are certainly necessary, but they will not be effective if the need to raise Europe's stagnant levels of domestic economic demand continues to be neglected.

The creation of the Euro has reduced Europe's external exposure and should have increased its policy autonomy in ways that allow it to pursue a more expansionary approach. But the political vision and decision-making mechanisms required to achieve this have been lacking. The Stability and Growth Pact has been gradually loosened in response to increased budgetary – and therefore political – pressures, but a more coherent and less reactive approach to managing Europe's economic affairs is essential.

One possibility was advocated by the Labour Party ten years ago when it proposed the establishment of a European Recovery Fund along with enhanced economic governance and fiscal coordination through the EU's Council of Economic and Finance Ministers. This was designed to allow for the effective regulation of demand at a European level. The European Parliament has put forward similar ideas for drawing on the European Investment Bank's lending facility to fund new infrastructure projects. These and other practical options for counter-cyclical economic management need to be considered once again if Europe is to achieve and sustain higher levels of employment and growth.

Britain's exclusion from the Euro hampers the labour movement's ability to contribute to this debate. But whether we are in the Eurozone or not, the only rational position for Britain is to want the Euro to succeed. The Eurozone accounts for much the largest part of our trade and many of the new member states are planning to join the single currency over the next few years. The further growth and integration of the Eurozone will mean that for profound political and economic reasons, the option of British membership must continue to be a live possibility and the decision on entry cannot be postponed indefinitely.

Europe's International Responsibilities

One area where the democratic Left should want Europe to make a stronger impact is in the field of foreign policy. The current imbalances in global power are incompatible with a progressive global condition and must be redressed as a matter of priority. A unipolar world order in which one country is able to assert its power and pursue its interest unilaterally is not only inconsistent with democratic values; it is a persistent source of international instability.

The emerging European perspective of international order is based on support for multilateralism, the rule of international law, global governance through legitimate institutions, solidarity between rich and poor, peaceful diplomacy where possible and military intervention where proven to be necessary. It is one that is today inadequately represented in world affairs. It will remain so unless Europe is able to forge a genuine Common Foreign and Security Policy (CFSP).

Europe must not only assert its belief in a multilateral world order, it must will the means to make it happen. Most predictions for the end of the unipolar era focus on the rise of the big Asian economies. On current trends the combined Gross Domestic Product (GDP) of China and India is expected to match America's within twenty-five years. But the European Union already matches America in the size of its economy. Its failure has been its inability to translate that into an equivalent political power, not as an armed juggernaut, but as a major influence promoting fairer trade, greater stability, environmental sustainability, democratic governance, common security and poverty reduction.

The near-monologue of existing transatlantic relations can only become a real dialogue if Europe is able to provide a strong, alternative voice. This is not to argue that Europe should seek an antagonistic relationship with the US based on rivalry – far from it. It is simply to point out that an effective alliance requires a measure of equality of power and esteem. It is no longer possible for anyone in the UK to pretend that equidistance between Europe and America is possible. Britain's long-term interests require us to prioritise our relations with our nearest neighbours, abandon any relationship in which we are perceived as a supplicant or accomplice and capitalise on our advantageous position as an influential part of a European Union that is capable of being an equal partner of America.

Europe's unwieldy and inefficient foreign policy structures need to be reformed and streamlined. The proposal of the European Constitutional Treaty that two existing posts – the Common Foreign and Security Policy (CFSP) High Representative and the External Affairs Commissioner – should be combined in the office of a European Foreign Minister was a sensible component of that and there is no reason to suppose that it contributed to the Treaty's rejection. The European Council should enact that reform at an early opportunity.

But there also needs to be a change in decision-making procedures if Europe is to develop a strong international role. Agreement amongst twenty-five member states will always be difficult when it comes to the most serious issues and a foreign policy that is confined to second order matters will fail to make an effective contribution. There is a basic and essential need to distinguish a single foreign policy from a common foreign policy. At the very least, there needs to be agreement that those in a minority will exercise a constructive abstention and save the veto for genuine issues of vital national interest. This could be achieved by political agreement without the need for a treaty amendment. The major change that is required is attitudinal. Each member state needs to regard the achievement of a common European position as a foreign policy objective in itself.

Europe must also keep the door to further enlargement open. The prospect of membership has been one of the most important

David Clark et al

factors in helping to sustain democratic change and economic reform in Europe for almost thirty years. It would be irresponsible for the European Union to abandon countries that are still struggling to make that transition. Ukraine, Moldova and the countries of the former Yugoslavia must be embraced as potential members, as should Turkey. The government in Ankara has already gone further than many expected in complying with European norms. It still has a long way to go. But it would be wrong to prevent Turkey from joining if it met the conditions for membership. To rule it out on specious grounds of cultural difference would send a dreadful message about Europe's unwillingness to accommodate diversity and the Islamic identity in particular. A prosperous and democratic Turkey would be a great asset to Europe as well as a great gain for its people. The democratic Left should therefore strive to ensure that it becomes a reality.

Strengthening European Democracy

The rejection of the European Constitutional Treaty has put the debate about Treaty revision on indefinite hold. But there are things that can and should still be done to make the European Union more open and accountable. The main problem here is not fundamentally a lack of democracy. The European Union's detractors may wish to ignore or obscure it, but the legal and political fact is that the decisions that count are taken by the elected governments of the member states, usually with the directly elected European Parliament exercising the power of co-decision, and decisions are often exhaustively scrutinised. This hardly adds up to a serious democratic deficit. The main problems are a lack of transparency and the absence of a genuine and informed Europe-wide political debate.

The first of these should be addressed by implementing the proposal contained in the Constitutional Treaty obliging the Council of Ministers to hold its legislative proceedings in public. It is not acceptable that the European Union is still able to pass laws in secret and while public proceedings are not the whole answer, they would provide a significant start. Whether this is done or not, however, the governments of the member states, the Council, the Commission and the Parliament should make an unprecedented and active commitment to informing the peoples of Europe about the nature, purposes, financing, management, operation and potential of the Union. In the absence of such efforts, widespread public suspicions about 'Europe' are inevitable and the opportunities for nourishing Europhobic sentiments are exploited.

A second step would be to open up the European Union's intergovernmental policy areas – the common foreign and security policy and justice and home affairs – to genuine scrutiny. The European Parliament has no powers in these areas and there is currently no effective oversight by national legislatures either. Joint meetings of European and national parliamentarians would have both the legitimacy and expertise to hold the Council of Ministers to account while being seen to do so. Given the rapid growth of police and security cooperation as part of the war on terror, a step of this kind would make a real contribution to strengthening European democracy.

What is really lacking, however, is the sense that European citizens are involved in a common political debate about their future. Politics has remained stubbornly national in its focus and even the European parliamentary elections are usually little more than an opportunity for voters to give their national governments a bit of a kick. This will need to change if the European project is to regain popular legitimacy. Among the options suggested is to proceed with the creation of a new position of Chairman or President of the European Council, as suggested in the European Constitution, but to subject it to direct Europe-wide election. It would be impossible to treat such an election as being about anything other than Europe, especially since voters in most member states would not have a candidate of their own nationality to choose from.

Creating an electoral opportunity of this kind would allow Europeans to have a meaningful debate about the options in front of them, including the sorts of issues described above.

Finally, the peoples of Europe may come to feel that European integration is something they take part in instead of something that is simply done to them.

Conclusion

The labour movement should be positive about the European experience and the potential it holds for a better world. Although the practice of European integration can certainly be faulted in specific respects, the creation of a transnational framework of democratic and law-based governance is a breakthrough in the development of human civilisation that ought to be cherished. If the European Union did not exist, the consequences of globalisation mean that something very much like it would need to be created. The nations of Europe no longer have the luxury of being able to go it alone, but they do have the opportunity – and the means – of acting together for their own benefit and to secure wider progress.

Moreover, it is clear that European values and preferences correspond closely with those that have always defined the democratic Left. As the American author, Jeremy Rifkin, has argued: 'The European Dream emphasizes community relationships over individual autonomy, cultural diversity over assimilation, quality of life over the accumulation of wealth, sustainable development over unlimited material growth, deep play over unrelenting toil, universal human rights and the rights of nature over property rights, and global cooperation over the unilateral exercise of power.' It is only by working together with the rest of Europe that we can hope to make that dream a living reality in the UK and across the continent.

The response to Europe's current problems cannot be to retreat into the politics of national isolationism or to narrow our agenda to the solitary task of creating an economic market. The peoples of Europe want much more than that and, in Europe, a high-growth modern market can only be achieved if it has a strong social dimension. Europeans want the opportunity to thrive in the global era without compromising their prosperity, security, freedom and social standards. Our ability to meet those aspirations has always been the fundamental test of our relevance as a political movement. It is a challenge we can only now realistically face as part of a strong and politically united Europe with a clear progressive agenda.

Some Reflections on the European Social Model

By Vladimir Špidla

The rejection of the proposed European Union (EU) Constitution in the recent referendums in France and the Netherlands raised difficult questions about the direction the EU should take. One interpretation of the outcomes of the referendums is that Europe's citizens are worried about jobs, quality of life and economic growth. In this context, reflection about the European Social Model is not only timely but of great importance.

The public debate around the social model often boils down to two opposing perceptions. Firstly, there are those who consider that the economic and social insecurity stemming from globalisation is a threat to the European Social Model. Europe, in their view, would thus be powerless to satisfy its citizens' need for security. Conversely, there are those who consider that it is the European Social Model itself that is threatening Europe's capacity to adjust to globalisation and international competition. Lack of flexibility in labour markets, combined with the excessive costs of social protection, is seen by them as an obstacle to economic efficiency and to essential reform.

But this does not give the full picture. Europe today has to face up to major changes – demography, globalisation, technical innovation – which are in the process of transforming society and our economies. Adapting and modernising the social model will therefore be a major challenge in the years ahead and this is the objective the Union must pursue. However, due attention must be paid to the legitimate concerns of our fellow citizens in Europe and action is needed both at the Community and the national levels to allay these concerns and misgivings.

The European Social Model Rests on Common Values

The European Social Model is based on a set of common values. These values are shared among all the member states. They are reflected in the founding treaties of the European Union and in the national legislations of member states. Among these fundamental values are the commitment to democracy, the rejection of all forms of discrimination, universal access to education, accessible and good quality healthcare, gender equality, solidarity and equity, the recognition of the role of the social partners and of social dialogue. These values are constitutive for Europe. In other words, Europe ends where these values are not shared.

The Role of Europe

Europe is not a monolithic block, nor is the European Social Model. The levels of prosperity, the traditions, the policy choices vary between regions and member states of the European Union. To some extent, Europe is defined by its diversity, which accounts for much of its richness.

The same diversity can be found when we reflect on the European Social Model. Here too there are several different concepts, different approaches and policy choices – in other words different ways to develop common values.

There are also shared values and shared elements stemming from integration. But in the architecture of the founding treaties and in the division of competencies between the national and the European level, employment and social policies are essentially of the domain and competence of member states. In the area of social policy the European Union cannot, and from an efficiency point of view should not, aim at playing the role of the member states. According to the principle of subsidiary, policies must be designed and implemented at the level that is the most effective.

Diversity in the Policy Responses

Member states are diverse when it comes to social systems and responses to change. When we look at the respective performances of the member states in coping with the challenges of demography, globalisation and technical innovation, we can draw some interesting lessons.

First, in countries with good economic and employment growth results, like Sweden or Denmark, social policy is seen as a productive factor. These countries have not been afraid to carry out institutional reforms in order to maintain their social objectives. Their overall approach combines economic performance and social cohesion.

In my own country, the Czech Republic, we made the difficult transition from a planned economy to a free market and had to rebuild a social system from almost nothing. The Czech Republic's growth rate was 4 per cent in 2004 and has stayed at a high level. It has managed to stay competitive and maintain social cohesion, combined with a level of poverty at 8 per cent, one of the lowest levels in the EU.

Second, the Nordic countries have also shown how a more flexible labour market can cope with change. In the throes of recession in the 1990s, Finland chose to innovate. The Finnish economy became more flexible and adaptable by investing in its human capital and taking up active inclusion policies. Combining flexibility with security and finding new ways of working was therefore vital. Flexibility was not only introduced and encouraged in the interest of employers, but also for workers, for instance to help them to balance work and family life through part-time or flexi-time work.

Equally, as the Finns have demonstrated, employment security is no longer about keeping a job for life. Today, security means acquiring the tools to remain and progress in the labour market. To become adaptable, workers must constantly be able to learn, first ensuring a solid basic education. Lifelong learning pays off – an additional year of education can increase a worker's salary by 10 per cent over his or her working life. An additional year of education also increases productivity for companies in the long-term, by as much as 3 per cent. Improving the quality of our human resources is also vital for the EU's ability to innovate. We need to become a leader in this area and can no longer be content to keep up with or imitate the latest developments in technology, even if we do this quite well. We need policies that will allow us to increase investment in research and innovation in order to reap the full benefits of the Single Market.

Third, the quality of governance has proven to be of fundamental importance in the process of coping with change. Again, the Nordic countries, but also Ireland and Austria, have shown the importance of involving the social partners in drawing up employment and social policies and in the management of change. The social partners' specialised knowledge and experience of workplace realities give them a crucial role to play, particularly in areas such as work organisation, health and safety and attracting more workers to the labour market.

The Added Value of Europe
European economic integration has always had a strong social dimension. The Single Market is complemented by the free movement of persons and fundamental rights like equal treatment and gender equality. Common legislation for health and safety at work and cohesion policy are important elements of the Single Market.

The European Union commands a range of different policy instruments to complement, encourage and reinforce the member states' social policy with the aim of enhancing the Single Market. There is the possibility of legislating at the European level in certain areas in order to minimise distortion of trade and competition between member states. There is the European Social Fund, which financially supports employment and inclusion policies of the member states. There is a long and successful record in fighting discrimination on the basis of nationality or gender and of encouraging mobility of workers. In the framework of the European Employment Strategy, the Union has worked with its member states to define common policy objectives and monitored their implementation, in order to allow for the dissemination of best practice. Best practice is also exchanged through the 'open method of coordination' in the fields of social protection and social inclusion.

Furthermore, in order to meet the challenge of protracted weak growth and the erosion of competitiveness in some member states, as well as to face and adapt to the rapid changes brought about by globalisation, it seems obvious that Europe must act in a coordinated way if it is to have a chance to succeed. The policy responses defined in the framework of the Lisbon strategy for growth and employment are of prime importance when it comes to sustaining the European Social Model – and thus command all the attention of European and national policy makers.

Safeguard the Values by Modernising the Instruments of the Social Model

When we try to draw lessons from those members states and societies that seem to succeed in the rapidly changing environment of today's world, we see that their social model does not act as a brake, but, on the contrary, as a tool, as a factor for success. In the uncertainty generated by rapid change, functioning social systems enhance flexibility by giving people the necessary security, the proverbial safety net, which allows them to take risks, to change and to grasp new opportunities.

There is no single answer to today's challenges. But the countries that succeed and achieve good results in terms of employment and growth are those that have undertaken coherent and comprehensive reforms tackling their social protection systems, their employment policies, their approaches to governance and the social dialogue. They have managed to safeguard fundamental values and foster a social model that is instrumental in enhancing competitiveness. These lessons should guide our work in the very welcome and timely discussion on the European Social Model.

Renewing not Rolling Back Social Europe

By Poul Nyrup Rasmussen

'Social Europe' Under Attack

'Social Europe' is a beacon of hope and inspiration to anti-poverty campaigners in developing countries with rapidly growing economies. For many people in Brazil, China, India and elsewhere 'Social Europe' represents an alternative to the individualistic, dog-eat-dog, free-market free-for-all that is held up by others as an ideal. It represents the hope that capitalism and justice and equality are not incompatible.

Yet 'Social Europe' is coming under attack. People say that with globalisation, increased economic competition and an ageing population, Europe will no longer be able to afford current levels of social protection. It is said that some of our current social protections – such as labour market regulations – are preventing economic growth. High levels of unemployment are cited as proof both that 'Social Europe' is failing and that Europe can no longer afford the same levels of social protection. Inequality is on the increase.

These are not questions that can be ignored. There are real challenges ahead. Times are changing – economically and socially – and 'Social Europe' will certainly have to adapt. Economic globalisation does mean increased competition, and there is real fear that if Europe fails to maintain competitiveness there will be further job losses and greater pressure on budgets, which in turn threatens to squeeze social spending. Enlargement of the European Union (EU) has brought greater diversity and inequalities of wealth to Europe and makes us question what constitutes Europe's Social Model. The consumer society has given citizens a taste for choice that cannot be ignored – uniform provision for all is not as acceptable as it once was. Demographic changes, our ageing population and altered family structures also demand different types of provision.

All these factors suggest that reform is needed. The question is – what sort of reform? We need reforms based on a new vision of social rights and welfare provision that matches the economic and social circumstances of the 21st century. People understood, and indeed fought for, the post-war welfare state with 'jobs for life' in a large state sector including many nationalised industries, basic universal health and education, increased access to justice and, in many cases, housing. But now people are less clear about what is on offer.

New Socialist Vision Needed

Politicians and business leaders talk a lot about the need for reform – labour market reform, tax reform, pension reform, insurance for health and education and privatisation – but no one offers a clear view of the guarantees society will offer. As a consequence, citizens feel insecure and uncertain about the future. The 'No' votes in the French and Dutch referendums on the European Constitution were symptomatic of that unease.

The welfare states were largely the creation of socialist and social democratic parties and it is that movement that must redefine the 'social contract'. Our vision of 'Social Europe' must enable us to make a clear distinction between the reforms offered for the renewal and modernisation of 'Social Europe' and the neo-liberal reforms offered by those who wish to roll back 'Social Europe' under the pretext of modernisation. We must renew 'Social Europe' and oppose those who wish to weaken or destroy it. We must avoid a 'race to the bottom' not only at a global level but also within the enlarged European Union.

Voters distrust neo-liberal 'reform'. Despite difficult times in Germany, voters did not give a majority for Angela Merkel's tax cuts for the rich or the removal of tax breaks for ordinary citizens. Even in Poland, where the ruling socialists suffered a heavy defeat, voters unexpectedly gave more support to the Law and Justice Party, which is suspicious of economic liberalism, than to the Civic Platform, which wanted to introduce a flat rate tax and speed up deregulation and privatisation. But socialists and social democrats must translate this distrust of neo-liberalism into a clear alternative and clear vision for 'Social Europe'. We must show how 'Social Europe' can once more become an integral part of the fabric of our society – not a luxury that we can only afford when Europe is booming. We must demonstrate that 'Social Europe' is not a cost to society, but an essential element of what holds society together.

There is a clear need for a new vision but the task needs to be properly understood. Academics are quick to point out that there is not one but several European models – some distinguish between an Anglo-Saxon model, a Nordic model, a continental or Rhineland model and a Mediterranean model. Obviously there are significant differences, but the similarities are more important – especially when compared to the US or Asia. Regardless of how they are organised or financed, all member states spend between 7-10 per cent of Gross Domestic Product (GDP) on health and 7-12 per cent of GDP on pensions. Despite the differences, you cannot convince an American or Indian that Europe does not have a unique system of social protection!

However, the sort of new vision for 'Social Europe' that socialists and social democrats need to paint for the citizens of Europe is not a 'one size fits all' system of social protection. Member states will continue to provide services such as health, education and income protection in a way that is appropriate to their respective societies.

Of course, there also needs to be a debate about strengthening the 'social *acquis*' – the basic social provisions that are required in all EU member states. There is a whole set of EU laws and directives covering social dialogue, safety at work, the mobility of workers and freedom of movement, and European labour market regulations.

Values and Principles for a New 'Social Europe'

Our vision of a renewed 'Social Europe' must be an articulation of common values and principles. Perhaps it can include a common understanding of the range and types of social policies required in today's Europe. A political and social direction is what is needed – not a blueprint for the actual provision of specific services.

It is not hard to identify some socialist principles that must underpin our vision. Solidarity, equality and justice remain as relevant and popular as they have ever been.

Solidarity means that everyone has the chance to access basic necessities such as healthcare, education, decent housing and the opportunity to work. It also means collective provision. Socialists, and indeed most Europeans, support this idea of collective provision: that everyone pays for services that everyone has the right to use when necessary. All health services in Europe are based on collective provision of one type or another – in the US they are centred on individual provision. Solidarity also involves a measure of wealth redistribution – within and between member states of the European Union.

'Social Europe' must also address how we deliver social justice in today's changing society. Universality is at the centre of our approach, and for this reason we must modernise social protection in order to provide it in today's world. The rise of new disadvantaged groups in our societies – like single parent families and second and third generation immigrants – highlights the need to rethink our approach to social justice and target it pro-actively at these groups for labour market and also societal integration. Public policies – in social protection, employment and education – must be modernised in order to address new societal issues, for example ensuring a smooth transition for divorcing families, a period during which many women and children fall into poverty.

Policies for a New 'Social Europe'

What are the sort of policies a new 'Social Europe' might embrace?

I believe 'flexicurity' is one policy that deserves wider consideration. This means increasing labour market flexibility while providing income support and assistance to get back into work during periods between jobs. There does seem to be evidence that this approach is more efficient than the very strong employment protection adopted in some countries. However, the Left must insist that any increase in 'flexi' is accompanied by real improvements in 'security' – income protection, training and support to find new employment. And 'flexi' cannot simply mean making it easier to fire people. It also means making it easier for people to enter employment – whether by providing better childcare facilities or by introducing anti-discrimination legislation. It involves active labour market policies, with concentrated investment in training and re-skilling, as well as personalised career advice for the unemployed.

It is becoming increasingly difficult for young people to make the transition between education and work. There is a need for more access to vocational training, workplace experience, modular education and credit accumulation – 'small steps' education and training so young people do not fall off the ladder.

I believe there is a case for a more thorough debate and comprehensive approach to issues of equality. Attitudes and legislative action on racial discrimination, on the rights of gays and lesbians to a family and working life, on equality for women, vary greatly. There is a need to take a look at initiatives on gay rights in Belgium and Spain, for example, and on racial discrimination in the UK and elsewhere. There are women in Europe who still do not have access to affordable childcare and do not have individual fiscal and social security rights.

There needs to be a calm assessment of the policy requirements of demographic change. An ageing population is not necessarily a disaster either for the pension system or for health costs, but the implications cannot be ignored. The third and fourth ages of life – which are rising rapidly in numbers – also require new, pro-active public policies for active ageing. Active ageing is not just about paid employment, but about maintaining health and actively contributing to society, through engagement in local communities and in politics. Falling birth rates can be tackled, and indeed there is evidence that women in countries with low fertility rates would like more children, and require better childcare, improved parental leave and a closing of the gender pay gap.

There is an urgent need to improve how Europe looks at, and deals with, migration and integration. Here a new EU common framework for admissions is needed alongside the reinforcement of anti-discrimination legislation and clearer rights and duties for migrants. There can be no new 'Social Europe' without a new approach to migration and asylum that combines solidarity and respect for the individual, a positive appreciation of the economic value of migrants and mechanisms for helping migrants to integrate and enter the job market. Here Europe should do even more than sharing experiences and building on best practice. Europe has made tremendous strides in becoming a multi-cultural society, yet the Right continues to exploit migration and integration problems to whip up resentment and undermine solidarity. Socialists cannot ignore the truth that dissatisfaction is high both among migrant communities and in many 'host' neighbourhoods.

Party of European Socialists (PES)
This is not a cry in the wilderness for a debate. In addition to the Informal European Summit on Europe called by Tony Blair under

the 2005 British Presidency of the EU, the Party of European Socialists has kicked off a dialogue between its member parties on how to combine social security with international competitiveness, growth and jobs in new and modern ways. Following an initial conference in Brussels involving several ministers and European Commissioners, and consultations between PES party leaders, the PES set up three forums for the different parties to discuss 'An Active Society', 'An Inclusive Society' and 'The EU Dimension'. These forums allowed us to share experiences and best practice, and develop fundamental common principles in our approach at the national and European level. The launch conference for this initiative took place in December 2005 and the PES congress in Autumn 2006 has been chosen for the unveiling of the comprehensive policy report to party leaders. As President of the Party of European Socialists I am proud that the PES is fulfilling its role to bring together the socialist, social democratic and labour parties of Europe to forge a new vision for Europe in the new millennium.

The Social Dimension of the European Union

Angelica Schwall-Düren

The debates about European Union (EU) enlargement and about specific legislative projects such as the 'services directive', and the negative outcome of the referendums in France and the Netherlands on the European Constitution have revealed a growing euroscepticism. Citizens' increasing reservations about the EU have many different causes. But it is their dwindling confidence in the EU's social dimension which weighs most heavily.

The concept of 'sustainable development', which was developed by the Brundtland Commission and adopted by the United Nations, comprises not only environmental, but also social and economic policy fields.

Based on this understanding of sustainability and the further development of this concept, the heads of state and government who convened for the Spring European Council in 2000 – most of whom were social democrats – adopted the Lisbon strategy as a political framework which views economic dynamism, quality and sustainability of finances and a high level of employment and social protection as complementary and mutually reinforcing policy pillars. With this coherent policy approach, the aim is to master the complex challenges arising in the 21st century and to further develop the European economic and social model. The Gothenburg European Council added an environmental dimension to the Lisbon process, and a genuine European sustainability strategy was established. Its purpose is to make the EU the world's most dynamic economy by 2010, maintain and further develop the European social welfare model and take into account the environmental impact.

The Lisbon strategy reinforces my belief that the specific feature of the European Social Model is that it focuses – from the outset and across various policy fields – on the impacts of politics and the market on the realities of ordinary people's lives (both current and future generations). It is designed to minimise the individual risks of life and accompany the individual along a path which inevitably leads to change. In other words, this model is people-centred at every stage, for it is geared towards the concept of society.

Globalisation
Increasingly globalised markets intensify competitive pressure. Favourable allocation of capital (e.g. the use of the cheapest labour at the location with the lowest tax burden) injects new dynamism into economic cycles. Overall, globalisation is associated with a higher standard of living worldwide, but this is distributed unequally between and within regions: regions with no access to the global market are becoming increasingly impoverished. People who cannot keep pace with the demands of economic dynamism are being forced to the margins of society.

The EU faces many different challenges:
- International competition for lower costs (taxes, wages, infrastructure, social and environmental standards), which, for

the EU member states, is mainly reflected in the relocation of production and business operations.

* This competition is reproduced within the EU through a pressure for lower taxes and wages; the integration of the internal market creates winners and losers.
* Worldwide and both within and with the EU, the aim is to secure leading positions in research, innovation and high-tech.
* However, demographic changes are also generating pressure for reform: a society with a decreasing number of children, longer periods spent in education and training, and a higher life expectancy has fewer people to finance transfer payments from wages, and must therefore find new ways of further developing this social model based on solidarity.

At the same time, the European Social Model is being subjected to ideological assaults. Neo-liberal economists and companies are attempting to capitalise on the competition argument in order to roll back democratic participation in the economy, weaken the trade unions, exert downward pressure on wages and reduce social standards. Even social democratic governments within the EU cannot always withstand this pressure.

Negative Mid-term Review of the Lisbon Strategy
The target set by the Lisbon strategy is to make the EU the most dynamic knowledge-based economy in the world by 2010, which means creating more and better jobs and strengthening social cohesion. The mid-term review presented by the European Commission shows us that this target cannot be achieved unless the member states step up their commitment and there is better linkage between the European and national reform processes. The improvement of the employment situation, in particular, is increasingly emerging as the practical test of political endeavours. Here, the EU is still trailing well behind all the employment targets agreed in Lisbon (total employment rate: target = 67 per cent, actual figure for EU-15 = 64 per cent; employment

rate for women: target = 60 per cent, actual figure for EU-15 = 56 per cent; employment rate for older workers: target = 50 per cent; actual figure for EU-15 = 40 per cent).

There cannot be cost competition between the EU and low-cost economic areas. If we were to push wages in the EU down to the level of India or China, people in the EU would starve. If tax revenue falls any further, it will be impossible to maintain or expand infrastructure where this is necessary. Infrastructure in its various forms is a key production factor, however. The EU member states must therefore resist the pressure to try to win the competition with business locations in East Asia through wage and tax dumping.

Competition within Europe

Tax competition within Europe must be viewed in more differentiated terms: the EU's target, among others, is to harmonise the living conditions of the individual member states (this will increase economic dynamism and create or safeguard jobs). This means that countries with a low starting point must have the chance to catch up: in other words, within certain parameters, they cannot be denied the opportunity to exploit comparative advantages, for they have disadvantages to overcome: poor infrastructure, a less skilled workforce, lower productivity, and often a high degree of environmental pollution.

Nonetheless, Europe as a location for business and industry will only be able to assert itself in international competition if its member states do not weaken each other. On the contrary: 'New Deal' processes must be organised on a joint basis. For example, one aim should be to strive for tax harmonisation in several stages: firstly, by making every effort to achieve a uniform basis for assessment (if need be, only in the Eurozone at first; initial steps have already been taken); the next stage would be to adopt minimum tax rates. However, this harmonisation only has any prospect of being implemented if the member states that are 'catching up' have successfully completed their adjustment processes.

A political commitment to the European model of society does neither just mean social policy nor is it merely a social market economy. It must be a 'social market economy plus'. That means that the political and economic actors must focus on the social dimension from the outset. A normative understanding of the European Social Model is undoubtedly required in this context. We must fight for this model in all its diversity, not only in theoretical but also in very practical terms. This means that a balance must be achieved between competition and the social dimension of the EU. The European Constitution would form a better basis for this process than the Treaty of Nice. However, this social dimension, alongside the internal market, must be the focus of all decisions adopted in the EU.

Economic Issues

Europe's single currency, the Euro, has been a great success. The independent European Central Bank (ECB) successfully monitors currency stability. Germany ranks at the lower end of the European inflation table. German companies are still performing very strongly in the export sector (indeed, Germany is world champion in this sector). However, the fact that the targets of full employment and a balanced budget have not yet been achieved by Germany – or, indeed, by several other member states – indicates that besides implementing reforms, better macroeconomic coordination is also required ('economic governance').

Until now, the Stability and Growth Pact has solely been used for the purposes of currency stability, while the conditions necessary for macroeconomic stability, economic growth and therefore more employment, have been neglected. The differentiated view of the Stability and Growth Pact which has now emerged must be supported in a sustained way by social democrats. However, there must be a place for an anticyclical policy during periods of strong growth as well, in order to create the potential for investments during periods of economic weakness. The ECB, too, must be urged to keep in mind the growth target, while at the same time not forgetting the need for job creation.

The Stability and Growth Pact rightly requires the member states' governments to pursue a policy of financial sustainability, but it neglects the growth aspect. The incoherence of the savings demanded by the EU also becomes apparent when the net contributors are paying more towards an increased range of activities.

Citizens also do not accept that EU subsidies are a factor in the relocation of jobs, rather than in job creation. Social democrats must therefore demand a reform of the EU's agricultural, structural and coherence policies. The years until a mid-term review of the 2007-13 financial period must be used for this debate. In the medium term, a further question which will arise is whether authorities at the European level should also have the right to raise taxes, in order to make the EU even more accountable to citizens for its revenue and expenditure.

A high standard of living for everyone cannot be achieved without a successful economy. That is why every effort must be made to create favourable conditions for this process. Reducing bureaucracy and assessing the impacts of legislation are the right means of doing this. Deregulation policies, such as those provided for by the 'services directive', should be designed to increase economic dynamism. However, they should not result in wage, quality and safety dumping. The European Parliament was therefore quite right to introduce far-reaching changes to the Bolkestein directive. After the European Council's welcome of the European Parliament result and following the modified proposal presented by the Commission, it must be ensured in the further course of negotiations that the country of origin principle only applies to free market access. As regards the performance and control of the service in question, the country of destination principle must apply. This is the only way to ensure that the high standards achieved in different member states are maintained, and that an impetus towards harmonisation 'upwards' is generated. Workers' rights, workers' participation and high social standards are a success factor for high productivity, e.g. in Germany.

The reforms required as a result of the challenges described above must be developed in consultation with all social groups. The only way to offer people new prospects, to equip them to take on responsibility and tackle challenges, is to develop an appropriate mix of measures for this purpose, thereby ensuring that people do not simply view change as a threat and as unacceptable. For example, the state, the private sector and the trade unions could work together to develop initiatives for 'lifelong learning' so that people who lose their jobs are able to find new employment offering a living wage very quickly. We can learn a great deal from the Scandinavian countries in this respect.

Sustainable Innovation Policies
However, the EU's ability to secure a leading position in the field of product innovation and innovative processes on a permanent basis will also be crucial in determining whether it is able to withstand competition. That means investing more than before in education, research and technology transfer. Here too, sustainability is imperative. The risks which have become apparent in relation to energy supply increase the challenges arising in this context. The recent energy crisis intensifies the challenges associated with a sustainable resource policy: an 'away from oil' policy must promote the use of renewables in order to maintain flexibility. Productivity must not be driven forward by expanding the use of nuclear technology – which still cannot be controlled – on a massive scale. Increasing resource productivity is the way forward (e.g. saving and substituting resources, increasing energy efficiency).

At present, the EU still invests too little in education and research (the figure for the EU-15 in 2003 was just 2 per cent of Gross Domestic Product (GDP), and even less in the Eurozone). The exceptions are Finland (3.4 per cent) and Sweden (4.3 per cent). Germany is one of the middle-ranking countries with 2.5 per cent. With the decisions adopted at Genshagen, the German federal government aims to achieve the 3 per cent target by 2010. Individual smaller countries cannot compensate the larger countries' shortfall. Centres of excellence and the formation of clusters will only be successful if the commitment is massively increased.

The lesson which must be learned from the findings of the Programme for International Student Assessment (PISA) and *Internationale Grundschul-Lese-Untersuchung* (IGLU) studies is that more resource provision must be coupled with improvements in quality. Social democrats must push for a culture of lifelong learning to become a key priority in our society.

Conclusion: Coordination of Social Policies

Europe will only be successful if the individual member states coordinate their efforts in areas of national competence. This is why the 'open method of coordination' has been created. This method is also applied in social policy. Here, the challenges of demographic change must be overcome. In Germany, the link between wages and the financing of the social system must be relaxed and other forms of revenue identified (e.g. citizens' insurance). Social democrats should conduct a debate on whether the 'open method of coordination' is, both in essence and in practice, an adequate instrument with which to achieve harmonisation of social standards in the EU. My question is whether all member states should allocate a minimum share of GDP to social security. This would enable upwards harmonisation to take place while allowing different social security cultures to be maintained. An unresolved question, however, is whether the quality of provision can also be safeguarded in this way.

This type of sustainability policy can only be enforced in the EU if a consensus is forged across national borders. And this cooperation will not be achieved automatically. Admittedly, such cooperation is forced through during long nights of decision-making in Brussels, but there is a risk that it is irrational. It must therefore be achieved through a laborious process of debate. In this context, it is important to consider whether we need even more intensive political integration in the EU. Social democrats and socialists must steer this debate – topic by topic, step by step.

Reflections on the Meaning of 'Social' and 'Liberal'

By Jenny Andersson

The search for a European Social Model, less optimistic now than it has been, can nevertheless be seen as a rapprochement between economic and social integration after the decades of neo-liberal deregulation, market integration and social fragmentation. The Lisbon strategy, full of compromise and conflict as it is, expressed the ambition of giving the social sphere a key role for the process of modernisation, and stressed that economic dynamism cannot be achieved without a more coherent interplay between economic and social policy. Social policy in the Lisbon Agenda is defined as a productive factor, as a prerequisite for making Europe the most competitive market economy by 2010 by investing in people, making work pay and creating virtuous circles of economic dynamism and social cohesion. The idea of 'Social Europe' stresses that the 'social' is, in contrast to the American model, an integral part of economic integration and of European capitalism.

This contemporary debate falls back on a longstanding European tradition of stressing the interplay between economic and social modernisation and linking social citizenship to economic progress and efficient markets. This attempt to bridge the gap between the 'economic' and 'social' is at the heart of European social policy discourses from their modern origins in the 'social question' in mid 19th century Germany. In fact, the historic meaning of the term 'welfare capitalism' in the European tradition, in contrast to its American equivalent, which stresses corporate social responsibility, is precisely that capitalism requires social intervention in order to be efficient, and that unregulated market capitalism leads to fundamental social costs and inefficiencies. Historians have shown that the very notion of the 'social' as a specific sphere of intervention rose in reaction to the idea of a social crisis in mid 19th century Europe. The idea of the 'social' was linked to the observation of the distorted effect on the social organisation of free competition and the elusion of social responsibility in industrial capitalism. Social reform was invented as a 'prophylaxis', a preemptive intervention into the organisation of production to counteract the rising social costs that were equated with a massive failure in efficiency. As prophylaxis, social policy was productive, an economic policy and not a philanthropic self-help mechanism. This was the tenet of the school of social economy or *Sozialökonomie*, which in the mid 19th century was formulated by German economists in explicit critique of what was then known as 'English economics' or 'Manchester liberalism'. The notion of the 'social' was thus given an explicitly economic function, and the origin of modern social policies must be located in the tension between the dual challenge of creating a basic level of individual security and laying the foundation for the efficient organisation of production through the allocation of social resources. The idea of social policy and social citizenship as in some way productive is therefore a tradition at the heart of the European project.

However, this notion of the productive effects of social intervention has taken very different forms in historic European discourses on social policy. The extension of the franchise and the breakthrough of organised labour saw the advent of rights-based discourses of social citizenship that broke with the conservative debates of the 19th century in which social policy was strictly speaking economic policy, concerned with manpower and not with individual rights. To these new discourses, concerned with the transformative role of social citizenship in the capitalist world, the idea of social intervention as having productive effects became a strategic defence of social rights as well as a normative outlook on how the economic and the social world should be organised.

This duality in the historical origin of modern social policies, between their economic and social motivations, has some important implications for the way we think about social citizenship and the social contract. The tension between individual social security on the one hand and the collective interest of economic efficiency, stressing productive participation, on the other, is often referred to as a Marshallian dichotomy between rights and responsibilities. Marshall saw the extension of social citizenship as being in a possible state of tension with the market and market efficiency, a tension that must be resolved through the matching of rights and responsibilities. This argument resurfaced in the 1990s through Anthony Giddens and others in a debate that focused mainly on the revocation of the responsibility side, imported and translated from the economics of the supply side. Marshall's distinction between rights and responsibilities can however be expressed in a slightly different manner, as a tension, in discourses on social citizenship across history and nations, between an outlook on the individual as a productive resource or as a rights-bearing citizen. These two sides of the social contract are of course intrinsically linked, but the balance between them is historically specific, changes over time in the history of European welfare states and acts as a line of demarcation between different and enduring European traditions of welfare. It is also a tension at the heart of the debate on 'what social model?', which attempts to bridge and reconcile the very different interpretations of this relationship that coexist within the European tradition.

Reflections on the Meaning of 'Social' and 'Liberal'

My ambition in the following pages is to consider what this means in terms of the 'social' and the 'liberal' and the current renegotiations of ideologies of welfare. Esping-Andersen, in his famous typology of welfare states, argued that the crucial difference between the social democratic and Swedish welfare regime and its liberal or Anglo-Saxon opposite, was the role given to the welfare state in achieving economic efficiency in the Swedish model. The universalism of the Swedish model, Esping-Andersen argued, was rooted in a productivism that identified social policy as a productive investment into society's social resources and into long-term economic dynamism. This stands against liberal conceptions of social policy as, ultimately, a cost for market spillovers. A Swedish outlook on social policy as productive meant that social policy was not, as in the liberal model, restricted to the residual role of dealing with the worst effects of capitalism on the social sphere, but designed as an institutionally redistributive strategy for decommodification and equality.

The question is of course to what extent such a distinction is valid today, after decades of convergence and integration, or indeed if it was ever valid. I argue in the following that it is valid, but the distinction between 'social' and 'liberal' is of course also to some extent a trope. In all fairness, Esping-Andersen's 1990s definition of Sweden as the archetypical welfare state was a rather generous description to begin with. The productivist universalism of the Swedish model was also economistic and disciplinary. The famous 'Rehn Meidner model' contained an explicit manpower or supply side orientation that identified individuals and groups as possible labour reserves and sought to bring them into production. The Swedish model contained a work ethic, built into the policies and institutions of productive universalism, that had nothing to do with administering handouts. It is reflected in the duality that is at the core of the Swedish welfare model, between the strong social rights provided for income-related social insurances based on labour market participation, and much more conditional entitlements, often means-tested, for the groups at the margins or outside of the labour market. In addition, it should be pointed out that the Swedish model has gone through a process of substantial change in the decades of retrenchment – and even if it has rather successfully emerged on the other side, certainly some of its veneer has flaked. For instance, the conditionality and increased selectivity that have found their way into Swedish labour market policies in the 1990s were framed in those familiar – distinctly liberal – discourses of incentives that structured the process of welfare state modernisation in the last two decades. In Sweden just as in other European countries, this has meant that an old emphasis on the political responsibility for employment and labour market has been increasingly replaced by an emphasis on individual responsibility, nicely summed up in the Anglo-Saxon term 'employability', directly translated into Swedish as *anställningsbarhet*. Employability is a discourse that shies away from structural explanations of labour market problems or unemployment, and favours explanations that fall back on terms of individual dispositions and lack of skills. In passing, what are the effects of such a relocation of social responsibility from society to the individual on the solidarity and reciprocity that upholds the welfare state? Recent research by Bo Rothstein and Eric Uslaner shows that whereas there is a general and strong relationship between the institutions of the welfare state and trust levels in Swedish society, one institution is universally mistrusted by those who have come into contact with it – *arbetsförmedlingen*, the employment office. Why? Maybe because increased selectivity and conditionality leads to stigmatising and frustrating encounters with a bureaucracy that, in the absence of actual jobs, is mainly devoted to the shuffling and reshuffling of individuals between programmes of reschooling, incapacity benefit and early retirement. Active labour market policies, some observers suggest, have become passive labour market policies, slowly wearing individuals out.

Britain, on the other hand, has in the period from the late 1990s seen an ambitious reform agenda on poverty and unemployment and major institutional changes in social and labour market policies, to the point where observers suggest that it has developed a new model of 'Anglo-social' welfare, drawing on the historical elements of liberalism but also on elements imported from Scandinavian-style welfare arrangements. The supply-side oriented activation policies of the New Deal are therefore suggested to be similar in content to Scandinavian-style active labour market policies.

Whereas it is clear both that there have been important convergences at the policy level and that, at the normative level of discourse, the meaning of 'social' and 'liberal' today is floating, there are some important reflections to be made here. Importantly, governments in both Sweden and the United Kingdom (UK) have articulated modernisation strategies in the last decade that stress the positive interplay between economic modernisation and social citizenship, give a clear role to the state, and defend the role of social intervention as an integrated part of a particular model of capitalism. In Sweden, this is conceptualised in terms of an intimate link between economic growth and individual security, and in the UK it is defined as a process of reconciliation between efficiency and social justice. Both these strategies give a specific and clear role to social citizenship in the process of economic modernisation. However, the role that they give to social citizenship in the process of change is very different, and it is worth highlighting since this difference lies at the very heart of the tensions embedded in the notion of a European Social Model. These differences can be expressed, somewhat stereotypically, as a distinction between an economic approach to the 'social' or a social approach to the economy: a distinction that on the level of converging policies can seem academic but that in terms of the normative foundations of the social contract is crucial, because it translates to the differing conceptions of the individual as primarily a rights-bearing citizen or a productive resource in the process of change set out above.

While the Swedish and the British model may in many ways have become more similar in the last decades, the central influence on New Labour's welfare policies was not Sweden, but the US. Policies such as the New Deal were based not on a Swedish interpretation of active labour market policies but on the American micro policies developed by the Clinton administration, which are arguably closer to an American tradition of workfare. There is a fine line, admittedly, between what might be defined as workfare and what might be defined as active labour market policy in contemporary politics. But let us consider this distinction; workfare makes social rights conditional upon labour market participation, whereas active labour market policies are based on the notion that social rights are the necessary basis for productive participation. Active labour market policies aim to bring out the productive potential of all, whereas workfare sees rights as an outcome, something that is earned in the workplace, and consequently gives the unproductive no or few rights. The productivism of the Swedish model was not a stress on responsibility or obligation, but a stress on the productive potential of all. Swedish discourse traditionally is not comfortable with the notion of responsibility but would speak, rather, of the right of all to be productive. Reciprocity, in this Swedish interpretation, was not about an exchange between rights and responsibilities, but about the recognition that individuals could find themselves in a time of need and that solidarity was a question of extending help with the knowledge that help would be reciprocated when necessary. The Swedish unwillingness to speak in terms of deserving or undeserving poor or indeed of welfare as a kind of contractual exchange relationship, reflects this idea of reciprocity based on the recognition of need, but also based on the presumption that everyone will participate in the labour market according to their ability, if given the help to do so.

In contrast, the British modernisation strategy in the last ten years has had an overall focus on strengthening the responsibility side of social citizenship, ultimately by 'making work pay', by strengthening the economic incentives that will induce individuals to work. The contemporary social investment discourse of New Labour differs substantially from Swedish productivism in that it focuses on individual obligation and responsibility, but does not emphasise the productive effects of the rights side of social citizenship. It is strengthening the responsibility side that is understood as economically efficient and consequently as an investment. This strengthening of obligation, in many ways, has been the very meaning of the notion of modernisation in the British reform strategy since the mid 1990s. Arguably, it is even the prerequisite of the British emphasis on reconciliation between economic efficiency and social justice – the underlying meaning being that growth and social justice can be made coherent ends, through a process of modernisation that focuses on strengthening the work ethic, understood as creating a culture of obligation.

Another important and prevailing difference between the 'social' and the 'liberal' model concerns the question of security. The Swedish Prime Minister Göran Persson insists that there can be no change without security, whereas the British Chancellor Gordon Brown repeats that there can be no security without change. In Swedish discourse, security is seen as a precondition for successful change, and the only way of making sure that individuals cope with structural transformation and that 'all come along' (*alla ska med*) as is the slogan of the 2006 election campaign. Contemporary Swedish labour market policies have been organised around a notion of flexibility interpreted as security in change. This reflects the historic emphasis in the Swedish model that insecurity creates inefficiencies and hampers growth, whereas security creates courageous individuals who, in the words of the Swedish PM, 'dare spend, be creative, criticise and have ideas in the workplace, study and raise a family'. Individual security, in this manner, is given a direct link to growth, productivity and competitiveness, and insecurity is linked to laggardness, unruly competition and fundamental inefficiency. In the UK this relationship is the opposite; security tends to be identified with what stands in the way of successful change, hindering dynamism and opportunity, and associated with reactionary vested interests and welfare dependency. In the British model, flexibility is about the individual willingness to constantly embrace change, and the capacity to adapt to changing demands for skills in the marketplace. Equipping workers for change by giving them the skills to keep up with a fiercely competitive world is at the core of the British 'flexibility plus', but it is far removed from the way that the notion of security in change, rhetorically at least, aspires to set individual needs and security at the heart of the process of modernisation, which, theoretically at least, means that individual needs for security also set the limits of the pace of change. Similar patterns are reflected in the shifting notions of responsibility between employers and employees. In the British model the predominant notion of responsibility is individual responsibility, while Swedish politics have attempted to strengthen the responsibility of the corporate sphere, for instance in the debate on the work environment and work/life balance.

The differences I have pointed out above highlight the ongoing renegotiation of meaning of the terms 'social' and 'liberal', but they also point out the extent to which the question of how the relationship between the 'economic' and the 'social' should be organised is a key source of divergence within 'Social Europe'. The social contract is, on the one hand, a question of the organisation of the balance between the 'economic' and the 'social'; it is of course also a question of the relationship between politics and the individual.

The prevailing distinction between a 'social' or social democratic model and a 'liberal' or Anglo-Saxon model that I have tried to outline in the previous pages is a distinction between two very different social contracts. One contains a social approach to the economic, which is about giving social citizenship a central role in the process of economic modernisation, ultimately also setting social limits to the process of economic change. The other, rather, is most accurately described as an attempt to reappraise the social in economic terms. In the Swedish model this translates to an emphasis on the role of politics to free individual productive potential by providing security, collective responsibility and strong social rights – whereas in the UK, activating individuals is, predominantly, about strengthening the individual responsibility to grasp opportunity and using politics to 'tap' the productive potential of all. British politics, then, have so far been closer to an economistic appropriation of the 'social' than they have been about setting in place a normative outlook on how the relationship between economy and society should be organised, which arguably is what the Swedish model is all about. To that extent, if there is an 'Anglo-social' model of welfare, it has accommodated the 'social' in a distinctly 'liberal' way.

These differences between the 'social' and the 'liberal' are not carved in stone, nor are they in my view dictated by historical traditions or institutions in each country, even if they are indisputably structured by such institutional factors. They are of course influenced by a variety of factors in economic, social and political history that go beyond what I am trying to show here. What is important however is that these social contracts are also dynamic and the focal points of debate and discursive struggle in each country. In Sweden the run-up to the 2006 election involved a debate on the role of individual responsibility and activation policy, while in the UK the idea of a progressive consensus has led to a re-examining of the values of the British model. At the European level, social and liberal discourses coexist in a similar state of tension and renegotiation. What 'Social Europe' is or will be is a question for our future. For this future debate, however, the historical reflection that I have offered here suggests a warning. A social model defined by the economy turns the world view of social economists – that the economy has to be controlled in order to create social efficiency – on its head. Rather it is economic efficiency that needs to be restored and the 'social' is left to be fine-tuned, restructured and rationalised. This is not social economy, but an economic approach to the 'social' that defines the individual first and foremost as a productive resource. Arguably the notion of 'Social Europe' is still closer to this economising of the social than it is to a genuinely social model of capitalism, which would involve giving a constructive role to the rights side of social citizenship and accepting the idea that this may mean setting individual social needs at the heart of the process of modernisation.

References

Andersson, Jenny (2004): A Productive Social Citizenship? Reflections on the Notion of Productive Social Policies in the European Tradition, in: Magnusson, Lars, Bo Stråth (eds): A European Social Citizenship, Brussels.

Esping-Andersen, Gøsta (1990): The Three Worlds of Welfare Capitalism, Cambridge.

Garsten, Christina, Kerstin Jacobsson (2004): Learning to Be Employable. New Agendas on Work, Responsibility, and Learning in a Globalizing World, Basingstoke.

Giddens, Anthony (1998): The Third Way. The Renewal of Social Democracy, Cambridge.

Marshall, T. H. (1992): Citizenship and Social Class, London.

Pearce, Nick, Will Paxton (2005): Social Justice. Building a Fairer Britain, London.

Rodgers, D. (1998): Atlantic Crossings. Social Politics in a Progressive Age, Boston.

Rothstein, Bo, Eric Uslaner (2005): All for All. Equality and Social Trust, LSE Health and Social Care Discussion Paper No. 15, London.

Steinmetz, George (1993): Regulating the Social. The Welfare State and Local Politics in Imperial Germany, Princeton.

Social Europe and European Identity

By Donald Sassoon

The defeat of the referendums on the European Constitution in France and the Netherlands may have surprised some, but since it is unlikely that the Constitution would have been approved in Britain, Denmark, or Sweden and since a constitution must be endorsed by all, it was doomed from the start.

Napoleon once said that constitutions should be short and obscure. The aborted Euro-constitution passed half the Napoleonic test. It was obscure, but it was also far too long. Ambiguity is a double-edged sword. It can unite those who want to be united and find something positive in the text – and divide those determined to unearth a negative verdict.

This is what happened with the proposed Constitution. In France and the Netherlands it united a disparate majority for whom the Constitution was either unimportant or undesirable. If unimportant the vote could be used for other purposes – such as protesting against one's government. If undesirable, there could be no loss in voting against it. Some wanted a more 'Social Europe' than what was on offer; others wanted to keep Turkish workers or Polish plumbers out; others wanted to warn their national leaders; and others were afraid of ceding more powers to what they regard as an unaccountable bureaucracy.

Did people want an ever closer Union? Probably not. Did people want an even more 'market-oriented' Europe? Probably not. Do people want a 'Social Europe'? Certainly yes – and unsurprisingly so since no one wants lower pensions, expensive healthcare, long working hours and lack of provisions for young families.

Yet there is no denying that the driving ethos of the Constitution was 'market' Europe rather than 'Social Europe'. Like all such documents the Constitution was, inevitably, a compromise. But the compromise reflected a political reality, a determinate balance of forces and the balance, today, shows 'Social Europe' on the defensive and 'market' Europe on the advance.

The winning idea, expressed by virtually all conservatives and also by many (perhaps a majority) of those of the Left is that the main impediments to economic progress in Europe are labour market rigidities and excessive social provisions and that deregulation and privatisation, within limits, widen opportunities and resolve problems.

Thus the neo-liberal view is firmly at the centre of economic discourse. It is the central global narrative of our age. In one form or other it is at the centre of political debates in China (under the ruling Communist Party) whose growth rates are astonishing (and worrying) the world. It is at the centre of politics in Brazil too where the President, Luiz Inacio Lula da Silva, leader of the Workers' Party, initiated a pension reform bill cutting benefits for retiring public sector workers and raised the retirement age amidst the plaudits of the International Monetary Fund (IMF) which approved a new $14.8 billion loan for Brazil. Not everyone is a paid-up member of the global neo-liberal belief; there is some feeble resistance in London, Paris and Berlin, but no one can ignore it. It sets the agenda forcing its opponents on the defensive.

There are variants of this discourse. The parties of the Left are less enthusiastic about demolishing 'Social Europe' and deny that this may be inevitable. They seek to find a half-way – I hesitate to say 'a Third Way' since this expression is no longer heralded with the fanfare of yesterday – between outright resistance to the constraints of globalisation and a supine attitude towards it. The parties of the Right are aware that it is difficult to win elections by undertaking to wipe out the social gains of the last fifty years. Hence the relative convergence between left and right.

There is nothing new about such convergence. It has been part of western European history since 1945. The difference is that the agenda in the 1950s, 1960s and 1970s – full employment and the welfare state – was far closer to the aspirations of the Left.

The debacle on the European Constitution provides an opportunity to re-examine what might constitute European identity. But first it is necessary to be clear about at least one thing: European identity, just like German identity or French or British, is not something that is intrinsically good. It is either something which already exists and one is born into. Or it is something one constructs for a particular purpose. Either way it is inevitably a changing and artificial concept. Identity is no indication of behaviour.

The difficulties facing 'Social Europe' are central to the problem of constituting a European identity. Even though everyone is reluctant to face it, identities are established – not exclusively but also – against other alternatives. 'The other' is a necessary requirement for the formation of identities. It does not follow that 'the other' must be wiped out, gassed out, cleansed out or locked up. One can perfectly well tolerate 'the other' or even be pleased of its existence. But one cannot be a Muslim, or a German, or a Jew unless one is aware that, in so being, one distinguishes oneself from non-Muslims, non-Germans or non-Jews.

Thus identities do not have only a positive sign, they must also contain a negation. Feeling 'European', whatever that is (and there is no agreement), necessarily includes an awareness of difference. The problem is that European identity is weak compared to national or regional identity. There are some good reasons for it. A commitment to a European identity bears the stigma of past feelings of superiority, of racism, of carrying a *mission civilisatrice* or the 'white man's burden'. Historically Europe is not just the continent of the Declaration of the Rights of Man. It is also the continent of colonialism, the slave trade, Auschwitz and the Gulag. To keep the good bits and reject the embarrassing ones would send us back to the ideological building of nation states.

European identity cannot be constructed without postulating a difference with other models. And who is to be 'the other' for Europeans? The xenophobic parties have already chosen the 'clash of civilizations' model. They are on strong ground. The Islamic world is an easy target: torn asunder by its own divisions, faced by a wave of extremism and weakened by a chronic inability to formulate a framework for the coexistence of religious commitment and secularism, it lacks universalist appeal.

In 2002 Robert Kagan suggested a new *mission civilisatrice* for Europeans, contrasting the general European 'indirect' approach to so-called 'rogue' states, moving from confrontation to rapprochement, beginning with cooperation in the economic sphere – and then moving on to peaceful integration. This was an extension of the tired notion of Europeans being from Venus and Americans from Mars – a sound-bite turned into a book – but it contains a grain of truth, namely that what Europe does is to distinguish itself from America; it shows a different way; it has a different mission.

Given the power of the United States as a positive model, above all the image of modernity it has offered for so long, it is difficult to imagine a stronger European identity being built without a clear demarcation made between Europe and the United States. I am not suggesting that anti-Americanism is the necessary and inevitable basis for the development of a European identity. In an interdependent world anti-Americanism serves no purpose whatsoever. But one can be different without being antagonistic. The price that a hegemonic country – such as the USA – pays for being hegemonic is that it constitutes both a model and an anti-model.

What Would be the Basis for a
Non-American European Identity?

It cannot be found in military and power politics competition. The military gap is evident to all and need not detain us here. The European Union has sought to establish a common position on foreign policy and at times it has even succeeded, notably over the former Yugoslavia (the Kosovo war) – but this was not a distinctive position since it supported an American initiative which was undertaken under the aegis of the North Atlantic Treaty Organisation (NATO) and not the United Nations, that is under the politico-military organisation which links the United States with Europe.

In matters such as the Middle East and notably the Israel-Palestine issue there is a common European position, but this is barely articulated and quite ineffectual. The relative equidistance between Israeli and Palestinian aspirations maintained by the European Union has no significant effect on Israel – who enjoys the near-unconditional support of the United States – and is of minimal comfort to the Palestinians.

The Iraq war constituted a particularly dramatic instance of the difficulty of establishing a common European position. The two countries which are regarded as the central axis of European integration, France and Germany, failed to aggregate the majority of European countries, even though opinion polls regularly demonstrated that a majority or a significant minority of European public opinion was against the war. Besides, eventually, all of Europe recognised and accepted, through the United Nations, the legitimacy and necessity of the US presence in Iraq. Those who were against the war were not necessarily against the occupation: there have been no massive protests and demonstrations in Europe against the presence of coalition troops in Iraq.

The majority of European states supported the USA. Some remained neutral and a few signalled their disagreement. Donald Rumsfeld, the US Defence Secretary, was quite right when he provocatively listed the members of the European coalition which supported Washington. This included, many members of 'old' Europe (i.e. western Europe): Denmark, Italy, the Netherlands, Norway, Great Britain, Portugal and Spain as well as those he quaintly called 'new' Europe, virtually the whole of what was the communist bloc: Albania, Bosnia, Bulgaria, the Czech Republic, Estonia, Latvia, Lithuania, Macedonia, Poland, Romania, Slovakia, Ukraine, Hungary and Moldova.

When it comes to the main issues in international affairs there is no single European voice, there is no European Venus to counterpoise to the American Mars. The only effective opponents to the American occupation of Iraq have been the largely Sunni-based local resistance. Europeans either despair (Blair and co.), or gloat (Chirac and co.). There is no European position, no European initiative, no European solution. No one turns to Europe for advice. International affairs offer few elements for the construction of a European identity.

What of culture? There are, after all, plenty of European Union (EU) programmes aimed at favouring a common culture; there are exchange programmes, funding for research. Europeans are 'proud' of their culture, but when they think of European culture, they think of national cultures. In any case Europeans do not consume 'European' culture. They consume their home-made national culture and they consume American culture. The 'high culture' of the past is largely European, but what of the culture of today? Take popular music. Each country prefers their own songs… and American songs (and the odd British ones). Thus in Italy the best-selling albums of 2002 were by four Italian artists (Vasco Rossi, Ligabue, Celentano, and Giorgia). The rest were British or American: Queen, U2 (*The Best Of 1990-2000*), and the Red Hot Chili Peppers (*By The Way*). In April 2005 the best selling single in Finland was *Taivas Iyo Tulta* by Terasbetoni; in Hungary it was *Elment az en Rozsam* by Balkan Fanatik; in Italy it was *I bambini fanno oh* by Povia; and in France it was *Un Monde Parfait* by Ilona Metrecey.

Everyone seems to like their home-grown singers, but hardly anyone else does. French songs do not make it in Hungary, German songs are unheard of in Spain. The Europe of popular songs is united by the sound of American music.

If one takes books or films, the story is the same. A few French or Italian films are seen in the rest of Europe but it is the Americans who to speak to the Europeans while the French speak to the French, the Germans to the Germans and the Italians to the Italians. There is, of course, nothing intrinsically wrong with this – except that the goal of a common European culture recedes constantly from the horizon.

The one country every European national knows better than all the others is the USA. Films, novels and songs contribute to this. But the media too play their parts. Elections in European countries are barely covered by the media in the others, though the French and the British get some attention. American elections, on the other hand, are systematically examined, discussed, dissected and commented. Such a degree of attention is largely justified: who is the President of the USA matters more to most of us, and for obvious reasons, than who is the Prime Minister of any other EU member countries.

We are on stronger grounds when we look at 'Social Europe' in its wider sense.

What is 'social' in the European nation states and what makes them different from the other two main models of advanced capitalism – the United States and Japan – are relatively strong trade unions and social democratic parties; but their powers and ambitions have been much reduced. Besides much of this 'Social Europe' is anchored to the nation state – by far the main source of identity. The European Union is not seen and cannot be seen as the foundation of 'Social Europe'. On the contrary it is seen as embracing the market above the social.

That the dominant ethos should be market-oriented cannot surprise any observer of the history of European integration. Its driving force has always been the abolition of intra-economic barriers and the creation of a single market with a single currency. Welfare legislation has always remained solidly in the hands of nation states. And so has taxation, the main instrument of economic decision-making and welfare provisions.

There are, of course, important social elements in today's European Union. These have had the positive function of enabling many on the social democratic Left to accept integration and give up their narrow and futile vision of building socialism or rather, as one should say today, social capitalism in one country.

The social elements of the Union, however, were always meant to be functional to competition. Their purpose was to establish a level playing field inside the European markets, reducing the worst forms of social dumping, ensuring the equalisation of the length of the working day or guaranteeing a minimum wage (though not the same throughout the Union).

The electorates of states with advanced welfare states do not wish (and how could we blame them?) to reduce social provisions. Their healthcare arrangements are better than those in the United States and so are their levels of environmental protection.

However, the countries with limited welfare states – this includes most of the new members – know that their unique competitive advantage lies in low wages, low taxes and low social provisions. They are forced into policies of further tax cuts and more privatisation. Social inequalities between the different member states thus remain a constitutive part of the European Union.

One day, it is said, when the economic gap between the more advanced countries and the laggard has narrowed – and only then – there can be a more balanced 'Social Europe'. Which means there is little that is social now in the European Union.

There is plenty of the 'social' in Europe but this is to be found in each of the member states, especially the older member states. It rests within the domain of national politics. It strengthens Swedish identity or Danish or French or German. It does little for European identity. Thus 'Social Europe' is on the defensive while Europe remains divided by languages, political institutions and culture. One would need to build up and develop 'Social Europe', to make it a model for the rest of the world. But the Left is desperate to recast itself anew. It does not

Donald Sassoon

wish to extend the model. It seeks to modernise it and, right now, modernisation still means Americanisation.

For most commentators the rejection of the Constitution (and, may I add, the ease with which this rejection, the biggest defeat for the cause of European integration in fifty years, was digested) was the clear signal that Europeans lacked a 'European identity'.

'European Identity' – like many nebulous concepts whose meaning is almost impossible to define – are warm, comforting words. Most people can be European and something else. Only a few strident nationalists fear European identity. And we all know where nationalism has taken Europe: mass murder, genocide, conquest, oppression. So European identity suggests a process where Europe turns its back on the bad old days and looks towards a future of peaceful coexistence between peoples who maintain their languages, and the more pleasing aspects of their national identity. In this paradise yet to come, Italians do not contribute black-shirted thugs who beat up their opponents or *mafiosi*, but Dante and Giorgio Armani. Poles forget what the Russians or the Germans did to them and learn to love their neighbours just as Jesus, whom many of them worship, told them to do. The British stop being arrogant and do something about transforming their drunken hooligans into respectful and sober tourists able to applaud with equanimity the football prowess of their opponents.

Yet the fact remains that the nearest model we have for the deliberate construction of a common identity is the nationalist model.

Can one construct a European identity? Should one construct it? What would it entail? The only model we have for this is the construction of national identity. This takes us back to the nineteenth century when history, then barely established in the academy, was becoming important. The romantic revolution had re-centred it as the master narrative where the people could read their own biography. Heroes could still be kings and queens but only because they represented the 'genius' of one's nation.

153

Historians, for centuries the lackeys of sovereigns, the chroni-
clers of lies, now acquired a 'democratic' role and, with this, an
important market. The British historians of the nineteenth century presented a rosy and entirely comforting view of the development of British history. It was the history of a succession of
intelligent reforms based on pragmatism. Even Cromwell and the
little unpleasantness that befell Charles I's head were drafted in a
story of constant progress towards greater democracy and rights.
An enlightened ruling class gave in to popular pressure just at
the right time, before the masses turned to violent revolution.
Unlike the rebellious French, the confused but well-meaning
Italians, the militaristic Germans, the hopelessly romantic Poles,
the British did everything right. The cliché still dominates the
British view of themselves and has been successfully exported.

In France too history was used as the pre-eminent terrain where
national identity could be forged. A people who did not know its
own history, it was believed, would always be at the mercy of
despots by whom they would be hoodwinked and cheated. The
people had to be told the truth about themselves. This was the
task of historians, the new priests of the secular order. On 18th
May 1846, the French historian Michelet, reflecting on the kind
of books the people should be offered, wrote in his diary: 'What
is needed for the masses?' The popular book *par excellence* he
concluded, unsurprisingly for a historian, was a history text that
would tell the history of France and, above all the history of the
Revolution. Two years later, in the midst of the revolution which
briefly re-established the Republic, Michelet wrote to his friend,
the songwriter Béranger, to say that, as the masses did not read,
it was imperative that the Republic organised public readings of
its bulletins, produced posters with easy-to-read characters with
illustrations and that patriotic songs should be sold by peddlers.
In his 1848 valedictory lecture Michelet declared that the only
way historians could speak to the people was by telling them their
history, what they had achieved and what they could achieve.

What is a common European experience? A mythology of
progress and a civilising mission (ignoring the heavy borrow-

Donald Sassoon

ing from the Orient, above all from China, India and the Middle East) is one. Another is a bloody history of warfare and genocide. One could stress the positive and tone down the negative, but, fortunately, this is unlikely. Having conquered their professional freedom, historians are not likely to tailor their lessons and their books to the requirements of a common European identity. This is not to say that it would not be a good thing if Europeans had a greater feeling of belonging together and sharing a common destiny – particularly as it happens to be true that the dissolution of the European Union would be a political and economic catastrophe. Indeed all the documents of the European Union are careful to add, whenever they mention the need for more coherence and identity to avoid fragmentation, chaos and conflict and to help achieve cohesion, solidarity, subsidiarity, concertation and cooperation, that it is also necessary to respect the existing national identities of the member states. Every minor 'cultural' proposal, such as that of providing access to European Union Institution Libraries (1995) claims that it is an important contribution to fostering the spirit of European cohesion and identity and that it will strengthen the sense of a common European identity amongst all the citizens of the Union.

I do not think a European identity can be taught. I do not think that one can make Europe a nation state of the nation states – which is not to say the slow and painful construction of the European Union is not the best thing that has ever happened in European history. What should be taught, and certainly taught more, is the history of other European countries. But let us not forget that most people's idea of history is not based purely on what they were taught at schools and university. They learn their history partly from the distorted recollections of parents and grandparents, partly from the inchoate references to the past they glean from broadcast news, partly from newspapers, partly from books (above all from novels) and, above all, from television and films.

Right now the typical history taught in schools in most of Europe consists of a fundamental pillar: the history of one's own country. To this pillar is added a smattering of Greek and Roman

155

history, allegedly our common heritage – a notion invented in previous centuries – some major events (Black Death, French Revolution), some major landmarks such as the Renaissance and the Enlightenment (usually heavily geared to one's own country). The first half of the twentieth century is present with the two world wars. The second half is almost absent.

The peoples of the European nation states have not chosen their nation. They have had nationhood and nation-building thrust upon them. Eventually they became British, German, French, Italian and Belgian. They may have felt Scottish or Cornish; Gascon or Bretons, Bavarians or Prussian or Austrian, Sicilian or Piedmontese. And many still do, but, eventually, thanks to a bureaucracy and an education system which gave them a common language, states which gave them common institutions, and thanks to wars, national anthems, sporting tournaments, Eurovision song contests, national broadcasting and a host of other initiatives, Europeans have learned to identify with a particular set of political institutions we call 'nations'.

The European Union lacks such mechanisms and few would want the EU to have them. We shall not build European identity the way French or British or German identity was built. But while it is true that the nation state is still the main focus of identity for Europeans, it is equally true that European electorates are angry with their politicians. They vote, increasingly, for 'anti-system' parties of the Right. And they abstain more than ever before. At the 2005 elections in Britain Tony Blair won, for the third time, a parliamentary majority which would make most of his European colleagues green with envy, but the actual proportion of the votes he obtained, 35.2 per cent, was the lowest ever in the post-war history of the Labour Party and, since only sixty per cent of the electorate vote, one could argue that he is the least popular Prime Minister in post-war history, helped by the fact that the conservative opposition was even more unpopular than he was. But the situation is not much better in other countries. In Germany the CDU/CSU obtained 35.2 per cent and the SPD a little less, but at least the turnout (77.7

per cent) was better than in Britain. In Portugal the turnout was 65 per cent, far lower than the first democratic elections in 1975 when the turnout was 91 per cent. In the former communist countries, elections no longer attract a clear majority of the citizenry. In Poland only 40.57 per cent of voters bothered to vote. In most European countries few parties get more than 30 per cent. Everywhere else and for a number of years, various right-wing nationalist and xenophobic parties have obtained between one-fifth and one-third of the vote.

The situation is even more worrying when we look at participation in the elections to the European Parliament (EP). Here the distance between electorates and European institutions is abysmal. It is not just that few people vote but that, at the election to the EP of 2004, fewer people than ever voted (voting is compulsory in Belgium, Cyprus and Luxembourg):

Turnout at elections of the European Parliament					
Member State	**1979**	**1989**	**1994**	**1999**	**2004**
DE	65.7	62.3	60	45.2	43
FR	60.7	48.7	52.7	46.8	42.75
BE	91.4	90.7	90.7	91	90.81
IT	84.9	81.5	74.8	70.8	73.1
LU	88.9	87.4	88.5	87.3	90
NL	57.8	47.2	35.6	30	39.3
UK	32.2	36.2	36.4	24	38.9
IE	63.6	68.3	44	50.2	59.7
DK	47.8	46.2	52.9	50.5	47.9
EL		79.9	71.2	75.3	63.4
ES		54.6	59.1	63	45.1
PT		51.2	35.5	40	38.79
SE				38.8	37.8
AT				49.4	42.43
FI				31.4	41.1
CZ					28.3
EE					26.89
CY					71.19
LV					41.34
LT					48.38
HU					38.5
MT					82.37
PL					20.87
SI					28.3
SK					16.96
Average EU	**63**	**58.5**	**56.8**	**49.8**	**45.6**

157

In theory, and here is the paradox, one might have expected Europeans – disappointed with national politics – to look to the European Union for guidance and leadership, but their anger against their political class turned into opposition against the pan-European project of their national leaders.

But why are so many angry or, at the very least, disappointed? Europeans have never been richer. They have never experienced such a long period of prosperity and of peace. Of course many are unemployed, but unemployment (at most ten per cent) can hardly be a major cause for the disaffection of so many. Britain, in spite of its relatively low level of unemployment, shows a lower level of political participation than elsewhere.

The European Union is seen as an irrelevancy, a side issue or, for some, as an obstacle. Perhaps it is not surprising that the European project has failed to conquer the hearts and minds of so many: to become central to political life the European Union would need far more powers than it possesses at present. But to acquire more power it needs the backing of Europeans. It needs to conquer hearts and minds. And this is the vicious circle – the main impasse – in which the Union finds itself.

First 'Europe' was an opportunity to make peace between Germans and French. This is still regarded as the finest achievement of the European Union. As the years go by this is less and less credible in the sense that it is less and less credible that the Federal Republic of Germany and France would have gone to war again had it not been for the European Community.

Then 'Europe' became an economic zone, the Common Market. An identity was established. Being in Europe meant being on the side of economic prosperity. This is the vision of Europe that worked. This is what convinced the British (just) that they should be in rather than out. This is what convinced the Danes (because the British were in) and the Irish (for the same reasons).

By the 1980s much of the Left (and eventually even the British Left) had rallied round Europe. This was partly because the 'socialism in one country' model which they all subscribed to had become untenable.

The EU has grown in size with successive waves of accessions. There was the accession of countries formerly under right-wing authoritarian rule but with market economies: Greece (1981), Spain and Portugal (1986). These continued to prosper and in the case of Spain spectacularly so. When Austria, Finland and Sweden joined in 1995, the EU was still a rich countries' club. Norway and Switzerland chose to stay out. When communism fell it was impossible to keep anyone out, but the Social Model was more difficult to defend, in part because the new members were rapidly jettisoning their own social model (constructed under communism).

At this stage one could have opted for deepening or widening. The slogan of the 1990s was both deepening and widening. This proved unrealistic. The European Union was right to welcome the ten new countries in 2004 (Cyprus, the Czech Republic, Estonia, Hungary, Latvia, Lithuania, Malta, Poland, Slovakia and Slovenia). And Bulgaria and Romania will follow soon. But for this enlargement to succeed it would have been necessary to give far greater powers to the centre than the citizens of 'old' Europe were prepared to concede.

Why is that?

Because the existing rhetoric of elections has become increasingly centred on taxation, education, health, law and order and jobs and these are still overwhelmingly national issues. Nor can these be turned into pan-European issues. It would involve an accelerated transfer of power to the centre – and this is something the electorates do not want. The construction of a common identity, above and beyond vague declarations to pollsters such as 'I feel European', will remain firmly ensconced in the land of dreams and not in that of reality – at least as long as everyone, the Left included, continues to subscribe to the idea that devolution and decentralisation are always good.

The Real Underlying Debate in Europe is not the EU Constitution but, Rather, the Future of Capitalism

By Jeremy Rifkin

Europe has plunged into a crisis of meaning in the wake of the repudiation of the European Union (EU) Constitution by voters in France and the Netherlands. At the root of the crisis is a deep angst over the dire state of domestic and European economic affairs. The neo-conservatives argue that the only way out of the current economic malaise facing Europe is to deconstruct decades of social entitlements, benefits and programmes that have come to define the European notion of quality of life in a socially responsible society, and unfetter the marketplace so that competition can run free. If Europe does this, say the neo-conservatives, the economy will grow and the people will prosper.

The socialists argue, on the other hand, that the unrestrained Anglo-American liberal market model, with its emphasis on winner-take-all, rewards the rich at the expense of beggaring the working class and results in a meaner and more bereft social order.

The Real Underlying Debate in Europe

In a curious way, what's really on trial in the recent constitutional fray in Europe is not the EU constitution, but, rather, the future of capitalism itself, not only in Europe, but throughout the rest of the world. An increasing number of Europeans are asking themselves whether the liberal market model or the social market economy model is the best approach to charting the economic future.

These events remind me of twenty years ago, when Russian Premier Mikhail Gorbachev, responding to grassroots discontent across the Soviet Union and the satellite countries of central and eastern Europe, initiated his famous *Perestroika*. Mr. Gorbachev hoped that *Perestroika* would stimulate a soul-searching re-evaluation of the shortcomings and failures of communism. His intention was to save the vision of socialism by reforming the toxic practices that had made a mockery of Marxist ideology from the very beginning of the Soviet experiment. His reforms came too late for a moribund system, and the entire communist house collapsed.

On the 20th anniversary of *Perestroika*, former Russian Premier Mikhail Gorbachev hosted the World Political Forum in Turin, Italy. The event brought together current and former world leaders for a kind of celebration and postmortem. Mr. Gorbachev asked me to deliver a keynote address on the state of Europe and the world two decades after launching the famous reform initiative that signalled the beginning of the downfall of communism in Russia and central and eastern Europe. Here is what I said: 'With the fall of the Berlin Wall and the death of the USSR, capitalism has enjoyed an unchallenged global playing field to impose its will on the world.' I suggested that 'perhaps it was now time for the capitalist camp to engage in the same kind of internal soul-searching debate about the world it has shaped and moulded in the interim years.' The reality is grim.

Today, while corporate profits are soaring around the world, eighty-nine countries find themselves worse off economically than they were in the early 1990s. Capitalism promised that globalisation would narrow the gap between rich and poor. Instead, the divide has only widened. The three hundred and fifty-six richest families on the planet enjoy a combined wealth that now exceeds the annual income of forty per cent of the human race. The three richest families – Bill Gates, Warren Buffet, and the Waltons of the Walmart retail store chain – enjoy a combined wealth that exceeds the annual income of the 940 million poorest people living on Earth.

Capitalist ideologues promised to connect the unconnected, bringing the world's poor into the high-tech global village. The promise has not been kept. Two-thirds of the human race has still never made a single phone call and one-third of the human race has no access to electricity, leaving them marginalised and isolated in global commerce and trade.

The champions of capitalism pledged to promote sustainable economic development and to conserve and preserve the fragile biosphere upon which all life on Earth depends. Yet, we continue to squander our remaining fossil fuel reserves, spewing increasing amounts of carbon dioxide into the atmosphere, destroying the world's ecosystems and habitats, threatening the survival of our fellow creatures and adding to the worrisome threat of global warming and the prospect of catastrophic climate change in the coming century.

We were told that globalisation, under the watchful eyes of capitalist markets, would create a more stable and peaceful world. Instead, terrorism is on the rise, travel has become more dangerous and the world has become less secure.

Our business leaders decried the deep corruption that permeated the old centralised communist regimes, while many engaged in equally egregious corporate corruption, bringing down some of the world's 'most trusted' companies, sending Chief Executive Officers (CEO) and senior executives to prison.

Neo-conservatives attacked the centralised power exercised at the top of giant state-run communist bureaucracies only to see them replaced by equally centralised power concentrated at the top of 500 or so global corporations who now rule much of the world.

Why have the two dominant ideologies of the Industrial Age so utterly failed? Because the central tenet of each was not sufficiently tempered by the antidote of the other, to create the appropriate checks and balances necessary to make a more livable world for everybody. The central tenet of communism is best expressed in the oft-heard aphorism 'from each according to his ability, to each according to his need'. A noble principle, to be sure. In practice, however, communism stifled personal incentive and created a form of paternalistic governance that robbed the individual of any semblance of autonomy, making everyone a virtual ward of an all-powerful state. In the end, no one was held personally responsible for their individual fate and everyone was subject to the dictates of impersonal state-run bureaucracies.

On the other hand, the central tenet of capitalism is found in the words of the Scottish Enlightenment economist, Adam Smith. In *An Inquiry Into the Nature and Causes of the Wealth of Nations*, Smith writes:

> Every individual is continually exerting himself to find out the most advantageous employment for whatever capital he can command. It is his own advantage, indeed, and not that of society which he has in view. But the study of his own advantage naturally, or rather necessarily, leads him to prefer that employment which is most advantageous to the society.

Smith believed that an 'invisible hand' ruled over the marketplace, guaranteeing that everyone would eventually benefit, if only the market mechanism were left unencumbered. Neo-conservative economists and politicians still believe this.

In reality, the invisible hand has turned out to be invisible in fact. Left to its own internal logic, the unfettered market leads not to a bigger share of the economic pie for all, but, rather a 'winner-take-all' end game. How else do we account for the fact that America's unbridled market model has resulted in a dramatic widening of the gap between rich and poor, in direct proportion to the loosening up of external controls over its commercial practices? Today, American corporate profits are at near record highs, productivity gains are unprecedented, and yet the US has sank to 24th among the industrialised nations of the world in income disparity – that is, the gap between the small number of very rich families at the top and the millions of working poor families at the bottom. Only Mexico and Russia rank lower. Meanwhile, America, which practises the purest form of market capitalism of any country in the world, enjoys the negative distinction of having the most severe poverty of any of the advanced industrialised nations. One out of four American children are currently living below the poverty line. The US also sports the highest crime rate in the industrialised world. Indeed, twenty-five per cent of all the prisoners in the world are currently incarcerated in the US. Two per cent of the adult male workforce in America is behind prison bars.

Is capitalism salvageable? Yes, but only if we are willing to have a frank and open discussion about what capitalism does well and what it does poorly. The strength of capitalism is, paradoxically, also its weakness. The market caters to the pursuit of individual self-interest, and is, therefore, almost pathologically innovative. Individual risk-taking, the entrepreneurial spirit, technological innovation, and productivity advances exceed any other economic system ever devised. This point, I believe, is generally agreed to by all.

But then, the more troubling question has to be asked, what does capitalism not do well? It does not fairly distribute the fruits of economic progress. That is because the logic in the boardroom is to always cut production costs in order to maximise profits and shareholder value. This means reducing, whenever possible, the share of the gains that go to workers, as well as cutting the expense of preserving the natural environment upon which all future economic activity depends. The result is a world increasingly divided between haves and have-nots and a biosphere seriously weakened at the hands of self-interest devoid of a sense of collective responsibility.

What is the answer? In a globally connected world, where we are all increasingly vulnerable to the behaviour of others and equally

165

dependent on each other's good will if we are to survive, the hope for humanity rests on creating an Aristotelian balance that encourages and stimulates the entrepreneurial spirit of the market, while simultaneously tempering its inherent propensity to run wild and concentrate more and more power at the top of global corporate pyramids. Countervailing forces, in the form of a strong trade union movement, a diverse and healthy civil society, and engaged and vigilant political parties, need to continually reign in the potential abuses and exploitation of capitalist practices by ensuring a just redistribution of the benefits of the market with appropriate social programmes and an adequate social net without, however, stifling market incentives. This is, indeed, a tricky balancing act. Ironically, as it turns out, rather than being at odds, we ought to consider capitalism and socialism as complementary 'visible hands' that continually balance individual self-interest in the market with a collective sense of responsibility for each other's welfare in society. If individual material self-interest is not tempered with a sense of social responsibility, society risks narcissistic fragmentation and the exploitation of the many by the few. If a sense of collective responsibility does not make room for individual self-interest, we lose personal accountability and risk a reign of paternalistic terror at the hands of an all-powerful state.

The social market economy comes closest to the 'visible hand' mechanism I have described. Unfortunately, the current economic debate in Europe threatens to polarise public opinion to the extremes – pitting unrestrained market forces against the bureaucratic dictates of a welfare state. The difficult task at hand is pursuing an intelligent and sophisticated course that maintains a balanced tension between the entrepreneurial spirit of capitalism and the social solidarity of socialism without either vision vanquishing the spirit of the other. We are, after all, each and every one of us, an embodiment of both spirits. We desire to pursue our own self-interests while mindful of our responsibilities to our fellow human beings. A reformed European social economy that allows both aspects of human behaviour to flourish is a model for the rest of the world to follow.

What is the Way Forward for the European Economy?

By Dominique Strauss-Kahn

The French 'Non' and the Dutch 'Ne' to the proposed European Constitutional Treaty sent shockwaves across the continent, as these two nations were rejecting the Europe that was under construction. Above all they voiced disapproval of a completely free-market Europe, for they feel that it affords insufficient protection against the risks of the new globalised form of capitalism. They also gave the thumbs down to an ineffective Europe, which although built around the economy, is in fact failing economically.

The verdict is beyond doubt. The lack of economic growth is chronic. Since the 1980s Europe has been one of the areas where growth has been the most sluggish. Between 1980 and 2000 the average annual growth rate of the 15 European Union (EU) member countries was 2.4 per cent compared to 2.5 per cent for Africa, 3.4 per cent for the United States and 9.7 per cent for China. Only Russia achieved a lower rate of economic growth with an annual drop in Gross Domestic Product (GDP) of 1.9 per

167

cent between 1993 and 2001. *Per capita* growth of GDP in Europe also remains weak, for during the same period it was only about 70 per cent of that of America.

This persistent deficit is a threat to the viability of the European model. The virtuous circle that was an engine of growth has turned into a vicious circle. Lacklustre economic performance has hampered the process of social redistribution, which has in turn held down consumption and hence growth. Environmental protection is also adversely affected, as many companies are unable to fund the investments required to reduce pollution in their production processes. For this reason, improvement in the quality of growth, i.e. the achievement of growth without damaging the environment, has become more difficult. The slowdown in economic growth has thus put a strain on social cohesion and the values of openness inherent in the European model. The very funding of the welfare state is under threat, as room for manoeuvre is reduced while expenditure increases.

The first cause of economic failure is microeconomic in nature since Europe has yet to see through the transition from a strategy of imitation to one of innovation. This transition was made necessary by the completion in quantitative terms of the post-war catch-up process. No further progress appears achievable though reconstruction and the assimilation of existing, mostly American, technologies, and economic growth now rests on technical advances and innovation.

This transition has also been made necessary by changes in contemporary capitalism. The old industrial capitalism was based on standardised production aimed at a developing middle-class consumer market, productive investment in known technologies, a stable low-skill labour force and financial backing from the banks. Contemporary 'post-Fordist' capitalism has all the opposite characteristics: a wide range of products with strong technological innovation and high added value, a mobile, flexible workforce and market-based financing. This transition has been forced on us by economic globalisation, which has increasingly put western countries in direct competition with the emerging countries of the south. This competition has become unbearable in labour-intensive sectors, where wage costs are pricing developed countries out of the market. For western countries, the 'only way out is up', i.e. by specialising in the most innovative products and services.

European countries have, however, largely maintained ways of working dating from the post-war period: large mass-production industries, investment in plants, concentrating education in the primary and secondary sectors and trade apprenticeships and a particular form of capitalism in the relationship between companies and their bankers, i.e. what might be called the German, as opposed to Anglo-American model. In an innovation-led economy, the main factor for success is Research and Development (R&D). The proportion of GDP invested in R&D in the 15-member EU was much lower (1.9 per cent) than that of the United States (2.7 per cent) or Japan (3 per cent). Only one quarter of the working population of the 15 member EU has graduate-level education compared to over a third (37 per cent) in the United States. Of greater concern is the fact that the United States' annual expenditure on higher education is more than double that of Europe – 3 per cent as opposed to 1.4 per cent of GDP. To encourage innovation, new entrants to a market should be favoured over existing operators whose size constitutes a barrier to entry. Organisation for Economic Co-operation and Development (OECD) figures show that this is not happening enough in Europe. The increase in the number of jobs in start-ups is much higher in the United States than in Europe: 12 per cent of large American companies (measured in terms of stock market capitalisation) have been set up within the last 20 years compared to a mere 4 per cent in Europe.

The development of the European Community itself was based on this traditional approach. The Single Market was designed mainly to encourage economies of scale, rather than to stimulate innovation by encouraging new firms. Laws on competition are oriented towards relations between large companies and are not designed to favour new entrants. Moreover, barely 5 per cent of the Union budget goes into innovation and knowledge.

The lack of economic growth in Europe also has macroeconomic causes. While the United States has succeeded after the rocky years of the 1970s in re-establishing price stability without any apparent cost in terms of growth, Europe has put in place a policy of macroeconomic stability that has held down its growth rate.

This explanation for this is three-fold. Firstly, it may be attributed to the procyclical character of budgetary policies implemented by member states. Their capacity to boost the economy in times of slowdown has been reduced by the Stability Pact, which limits the deficit to 3 per cent of GDP. Secondly, Europe, or at least the Eurozone, appears to have a less reactive monetary policy than the American Federal Reserve. Thirdly, and most importantly, the inadequacy of European macroeconomic policy derives from an absence of a Union-wide policy mix. This virtually total absence of coordination of economic policy among member states of the Eurozone tends to cancel out the benefits of the single currency. Moreover, this situation makes any coherent discussion with the European Central Bank (ECB) impossible. Those who hold macroeconomic power in Europe thus do not work together, whereas in the United States, the Treasury and the Federal Reserve cooperate to decide on macroeconomic strategy.

This is now the economic priority for Europe. Before seeking to relaunch a political Europe of the future, we have to make Europe economically successful today. We need to base economic development in Europe on solidarity and sustainable growth.

What are the ways forward?

Fiscal and Social Competition:
A Scourge that must be Banished
This lack of growth is better dealt with by Europe as a whole than through any of the member states acting separately. Yet European countries have chosen to approach the problem in divergent ways that have brought them into competition to attract economic activity to their national territory, which turns into a race to be the 'lowest bidder' in terms of tax breaks and social legislation.

One tactic is to lower corporation tax, which has been cut from 50 per cent to 33 per cent in France over a period of 10 years, and reduced to a mere 25 per cent in Germany and 10 per cent in Ireland while there is none at all in Estonia. This crazy rivalry erodes the bases on which the funding of social protection and environmental policy rests and could easily, were it allowed to go unchecked, cause European countries to abandon their model of social justice in favour of a more strongly free-market approach.

An even more alarming development in this competition to attract business is the setting up of 'tax havens' for multinationals. Some member states have allowed large international groups exemption from national taxation and other advantages if they set up company or financial headquarters on their national territory. This is a purely European phenomenon, which led to relocations and diverting of investment within the 15 member European Union. These fiscal regimes, which apply only to 'stowaway passengers', decrease tax revenues without bringing any comparable benefits to the countries that implement them since all member states are acting in similar fashion.

Europe Must Invest Massively in the Future to Achieve the Ambitious Targets of the Lisbon Strategy

In order to achieve the transition to a knowledge economy, Europe must invest in research, innovation and education, since that is where most of its future will be played out. Given the cost differentials between EU companies and their competitors in emerging countries, no strategy based on competitive pricing can succeed.

The comparative advantages that emerging countries enjoy as regards production costs will not, however, remain forever. For instance, the economic development of southeast Asia will gradually lead to production costs becoming aligned to western levels. The current economic structures of the EU have undergone painful changes to achieve the transition that is now reaching completion but they will not be able to resist the infinitely greater pressure resulting from competition from countries with such large populations as China and India. For this reason, the

171

only viable strategy is one of innovation, based on knowledge and the re-orienting of economic activity towards innovative products and services. This is the only strategy that will enable Europe, as is the case for the United States, to make the technological breakthroughs that will allow it to complement rather than compete with the South. It is a matter of urgency. Production sites and certain services (call centres, accounts) are already being transferred to emerging countries and this could lead in the future to the delocalisation of research and development activities to emerging countries, for which, given their investment in education and training, e.g. in China, they provide a favourable environment.

Yet it is a matter of concern that Europe is falling behind in R&D. In order to keep up it has set itself the objective of investing 3 per cent of GDP into research each year, with 1 per cent in the public and 2 per cent in the private sector. This level of 3 per cent is based on best practice in western countries, yet it must be considered as a minimum if we are to achieve the ambitions of the Lisbon programme and become the world's most dynamic economy by 2010. Currently the 25 members of the EU devote only 1.9 per cent of their GDP to research. The Union can make up lost ground in R&D, if three types of reform are implemented. Firstly, R&D must become a priority within the EU budget. Europe must set itself the clear objective of becoming the area that invests the most in R&D. This requires that the EU take on a much more active role and that it set aside a budget equivalent of 0.25 per cent of the Community's GDP for research each year. In time, this Community-wide effort on public-funded research could go on increasing until it becomes, in terms of volume, the primary policy of the EU. Secondly, public-funded research must become more effective and funds must be correctly allocated. The setting up of a European research agency would help to increase the qualitative impact of the public funding of research by basing the awarding of grants on scientific criteria and not, as still often happens today, on geographical considerations such as the expectation of a fair proportion being awarded to contributing countries through the Community policy on R&D. Thirdly, too little money is invested in private research in Europe. The EU could encourage the setting up of tax credits for R&D and for innovative investments, for this is the most appropriate instrument for stimulating private research through a European Council resolution, or indeed by fixing a minimum level of tax relief for the whole of Europe through a framework law.

An economy of innovation requires at the same time a massive investment in higher education. As the EU has achieved full participation in secondary education it must now seek to increase participation in Higher Education (HE), which is indispensable for bringing about the transition to an economic model based on knowledge and innovation. There is, however, a major gap between the United States and Europe as regards HE, with the USA having 50 per cent more graduates than the EU. Nor can any individual country match the US in this area. This gap derives from the different levels of investment in HE, with America devoting 3 per cent of national income compared to 1.4 per cent for Europe. Even public funding is higher in USA, 1.4 per cent of GDP compared to 1.1 per cent in Europe. The rapid achievement of mass participation in university education is a major challenge for Europe, and first and foremost for individual member states since HE is their responsibility. The EU can, however, help increase European funding for this area, firstly, by setting the objective to be reached through a European Council resolution, i.e. 50 per cent of the population completing a course of study in HE; and secondly, by investing in a network of university centres of excellence which can seek to become world leaders in their specialisms. It is reasonable to plan that the EU will devote 0.15 per cent of its GDP to quality Higher Education.

Boosting the European Economy also Requires a Community-wide Industrial Policy to Combat Deindustrialisation and Maintain the Attractiveness of Europe as a Business Location
Industrial policy is not currently part of the Community's brief and the only elements we do have concern laws on competition. Economic Europe has been built in an inward-looking manner to

bring down national barriers in order to create a single European economic area. Globalisation and the dangers of delocalisation now force us to look outward in order to maintain the industrial competitiveness of Europe in an environment where international competition has increased. Europe cannot resign herself to a gradual depletion of all her industry, for industry possesses potential for future growth. Even in a service-dominated economy, productivity gains come from industry.

Loss of industry does not only mean delocalisation, although it is the most visible and socially painful manifestation of it. When a firm, whether European or from outside the Community, chooses to invest outside Europe (even without relocating a production site) it contributes to the depletion of Europe's industrial base. The problem must therefore be seen in the wider perspective of Europe's capacity as a business location for attracting international investment. In competing for such investments, Europe has three rivals who must be countered with different strategies. In the face of competition from emerging countries, Europe must invest in knowledge. In order to compete with developed economies, and in particular with the United States, Community law on competition must be modified so that European players with the critical mass necessary in the world market can be formed and not simply, as presently, to maintain competition between European companies in each national market segment. In the face of competition from within Europe itself, unfair tax regimes must be banned by law by extending the principle of equality of treatment, which prohibits 'negative discrimination' arising from the positive discrimination inherent in such regimes.

The transition to an economy of innovation requires that the Single Market become more dynamic. This can be achieved through three types of reform: firstly, the entry of new firms into the market must be facilitated, since new entrants or startups bring in innovations. This implies a refocusing of European policies on market regulation and competition which were not designed for such a purpose. Secondly, the Single Market must be complemented by a genuinely unified labour market. Thirdly, the physical unity of the Single Market has to be strengthened. The costs of improving European transport networks have been estimated at 500 billion Euro over the next 10 years, or 50 billion Euro per year. The European Union could cover between a quarter and a half of this expenditure. This would mean that the proportion of Community budget spent on infrastructure would rise to between 0.125 per cent and 0.25 per cent of GDP compared to current levels of under 0.1 per cent.

Boosting the European Economy also Requires Reform of our Macroeconomic Framework, i.e. the Setting up of an Actively Managed Economic Policy

In the macroeconomic domain, the malfunctions of the management of the Eurozone are now obvious: pro-cyclical budget policy, the relative lack of dynamism in monetary policy and an absence of policy mix. The weak reaction to the rise in the value of the Euro is a recent example. These malfunctions fuel the disenchantment felt by an increasing number of European citizens as regards the single currency. It will not be enough to adjust the instruments of economic policy in the Eurozone; the philosophy underlying European macroeconomic management has to change. That its management has been so loosely coordinated up to now is a consequence of the EU contenting itself with a kind of 'automatic pilot' based on a set of mechanically applied rules, particularly as regards budgetary policy. Although necessary during the period of convergence of European economies and absolutely vital for preventing overspends, this form of management is not appropriate when the objective is to restore growth and develop the job market. Closer coordination of economic policy has thus become unavoidable. It is therefore time to reform the macroeconomic framework of the EU and to reinforce the rules by active political monitoring.

This applies to budgetary policy. The weakness of the current economic government of the Eurozone is largely due to the informal status of the Eurogroup – the forum which brings together the finance ministers of the countries that have adopted the Euro. Since it cannot take a decision with the force of law, its coordinating role has never really developed, resulting in a lack of direction for the Eurozone. It has neither a common budgetary strategy nor an effective dialogue with the European Central Bank. This deficiency results in obvious weaknesses: inappropriate policy mix, an exchange rate dictated by the dollar and the absence of a united front and a strong voice for the Eurozone to the rest of the world. The Eurogroup must be given formal institutional status with full legal powers to decide the economic policy of the Eurozone, introducing consultation on the budget and exchange policy and dialogue with the ECB to define the policy mix, and prepare common positions on issues in international forums. It also needs a stable presidency with the elected president serving as European Finance Minister.

More active management of monetary policy is also necessary since the ECB acts as a brake on growth because of its preoccupation with price stability. The objectives of growth and job creation could be pursued without changes to statutes and in cooperation with other central banks.

Changing the statutes of the ECB would, however, send out a strong signal politically. It would not mean revoking its independent status, which is now common to all major democracies. The revision would come down to including in its statutes the fact that economic growth and job creation need to be taken into account. This would bring them into line with those of other western countries, in particular the American Federal Reserve and the Bank of England, which have proved their effectiveness.

Conclusion: Creating the Conditions for Development to Benefit the Whole of Europe

Here are the principle proposals for boosting the European economy: investing massively in the future; putting in place a common European industrial policy; setting up economic governance by granting formal institutional status to the Eurogroup;

ensuring that the European Central Bank takes on board the objectives of growth and job creation.

Such a boost is essential since without growth it is impossible to maintain the level of social protection that is the hallmark of the European model. The reforms that I have suggested here will facilitate the transition to a knowledge economy and revitalise the philosophy of macroeconomic management in Europe and thus constitute a strong foundation for sustainable growth and development to the benefit of all countries in Europe.

References

IMF (2002): World Economic Outlook, Washington DC.

OECD (2005): Education at a glance, Paris.

Sapir, André, et al (2004): An agenda for a growing Europe, Oxford.

What is the Progressive Case for Gender Equality?

By Zita Gurmai

Gender equality is rising up the political agenda. With emerging demographic problems of ageing societies, low birth rates and the subsequent onset of shrinking labour markets, politicians and economists from left to right are coming to the realisation that not only do we need more women to work, but we also need more women to have more children.

Feminists have been making the social justice argument for gender equality for many decades. In a condensed form, this argument goes something like this: women are equal to men, they deserve to be treated accordingly in all spheres of life – social, economic and political, private and public. This is an irrefutable truth but unfortunately only in some parts of the world has this argument achieved concrete results. My argument in this article is that the progressive case for gender equality currently carries more weight if it combines the social justice and the economic case rather than solely focusing on the social justice case.

What is the Progressive Case for Gender Equality?

I will focus exclusively on women in the labour market, what is known in the jargon as women's economic empowerment. There are profound gender equality problems elsewhere in society (violence against women including trafficking and prostitution) and politics (low representation of women) that I will not deal with here. Achieving greater gender equality in one area has positive spill-over effects in other areas and such achievements are mutually reinforcing. It is no coincidence that high levels of representation for women in the Swedish parliament (the highest in Europe, with women making up 45 per cent of MPs) go hand in hand with a high level of female participation in the economy (70 per cent).

The jury is still out as to what exactly the progressive case for gender equality is. It is much easier for social democrats to define the anti-progressive case than to pin down and agree on the progressive case. As Magdalena Andersson cogently argues 'progressive politics has an obligation to fight old-fashioned structures'. I will explore how some policies that claim to be 'progressive' are still operating within the parameters of these old-fashioned structures, instead of aspiring to overturn them.

Over the last few decades, in some parts of Europe, there has been significant progress in achieving the greater economic independence of women and in particular higher participation levels of women in the labour market. However, this progress is unevenly spread and the disparity with men's employment and earnings is still glaringly apparent. In the European Union (EU) of 25 member states, the average female employment rate stands at 55.7 per cent, whilst over 70 per cent of men are in employment. In every member state the employment rate of men is higher than that of women. The smallest employment gap (the difference between percentage of men and women in work) is found in Sweden (2 per cent), the largest in Malta (over 40 per cent). Moreover, the gender pay gap remains stubbornly high and shows no signs of closing. On average in the EU women earn 15 per cent less for every hour worked than men. This reaches higher levels in countries with higher participation rates. Ironically, it are the countries with low percentages of women in work which make this average lower than would otherwise be the case. Women are concentrated in low-paid sectors even in the most gender equal societies, such as Denmark and Sweden. Part-time employment also affects women's earnings, with 32.6 per cent of women workers in part-time work compared to 7.4 per cent of men.

Given the status quo of gender equality in the labour market, why is the most effective case for gender equality orientated towards economic considerations? Europe is faced with huge demographic challenges, an ageing population that is due to decline from 2025 onwards. It is not unusual to read headlines alerting readers to 'Europe's demographic time bomb' and 'rapidly shrinking labour forces'. Academics from different disciplines have been warning us about a potential demographic decline for many years but the rest of the world has only recently been slowly waking up to the reality of it. This is coupled with sluggish growth in many parts of Europe.

This is where the economic case for gender equality becomes so powerful. In terms of economic efficiency, it simply does not make sense to waste the potential of half of the workforce. This case becomes much more urgent against the backdrop of Europe's current demographic challenges. An ageing population has implications for the public purse. Our economies and welfare states are not sustainable if there are more people in retirement and fewer people in work unless there is pension reform, an increase in birth rates and an increase in the numbers of people in employment. Women hold the the key to two out of three of these solutions.

However, this puts several demands on women: to work more, to have more children and in an ageing society the burden for caring for elderly relatives often falls on women. Therefore the key element of a progressive view of gender equality is that women and men should be enabled by the state to combine work with parenthood.

Statistics show a new phenomenon emerging. We today observe a positive correlation between fertility and women's employment rates. High fertility countries also have high employment rates for women. Notably in the Scandinavian countries, high levels of employment go hand in hand with high fertility rates. Work has become the pre-condition for having children.

In an ever-increasingly globalised world of permanent change, in countries where women are not able to combine work and family commitments, they are choosing work over having children. Southern European countries with traditional gender roles have not been able to deal with the economic uncertainties of globalisation and have some of the lowest fertility rates in Europe. Evidence shows us that in those countries women would like to have more children. There is a baby gap between the number of children desired and achieved. Women are delaying having children with the average age of women at the birth of their first child rising steadily in all EU countries.

Having children has huge implications for a mother's employment, careers prospects and life-time earnings. Recent statistics show that having children decreases the employment rate of women by as much as 14.3 points, whereas it has the reverse effect of driving up men's employment rates by 5.6 points. Moreover, women with children are more likely to be in part-time work than men or women without children. One third of women with one child and half of women with three or more children work part-time. The number of children has no perceivable effect on men working part-time.

Gøsta Esping-Andersen underlines that the differences between the opportunity cost for lifetime earnings for women with children is larger in some countries than others. In the United Kingdom (UK), it is estimated that a woman with two children will forgo approximately 50 per cent of her potential cumulated life-time earnings; in contrast in Denmark there is hardly any significant loss in life-time earnings. As he rightly points out, a loss of a woman's earnings does not only affect her adversely but also her family which has higher risks of household poverty if she is not in work.

The policy mix for enabling men and women, fathers and mothers, to combine work and family commitments must contain three essential elements: universal, affordable childcare provision, shared parental leave and the changing role of men.

Firstly, the lack of childcare provision in the vast majority of member states also makes it economically unviable for one of the parents to work. For example in Spain the cost of a full year of quality care is equal to a third of an average woman's income. In a small minority of member states childcare is heavily subsidised, which enables both parents to combine work and family life. Gøsta Esping-Andersen provides a strong case for investing in universal and affordable childcare by showing in a cost-benefit analysis that the medium-term returns of such an investment far outweigh the short-term. However, the problem for governments is that their electorates judge them on short-term, rather than medium, term achievements. However, there is an immediate economic gain in terms of job creation. Esping-Andersen predicts a job multiplier effect: for every 100 jobs that women are enabled to keep or go back to, 10 jobs are created in the service economy (carers, cleaners etc).

Secondly, the right balance has to be struck for leave entitlements. If parental leave is too long, the chances of discrimination against women increase and employers are unlikely to invest in the skills of women of childbearing age. If parental leave is too short, there is an increased probability that the mother will decide to stay at home longer and thus lose her connection with the labour market. Provisions in some member states have tried to encourage men to take their share of parental leave. Some feminists argue that this is the only way to fight discrimination in the labour market. Men of childbearing age will thus be regarded as having the same risks (in terms of taking leave provisions) as women. However, we are a long way from that situation. A recent Eurobarometer survey found that 75 per cent of men were aware of their right to take parental leave but 85 per cent said that they would not take it. Even in the deeply progressive and social democratic country of Sweden only 15 per cent of men take up parental leave. Various factors account for this widespread reluctance. Stereotypes certainly contribute as does the lack or loss of remuneration in some countries during parental leave. The persistence of the gender pay gap contributes to this phenomenon in cases in which the father earns more than the mother. Parental leave schemes that encourage the father to take up part of the leave (in Iceland half the parental leave will be lost if the father does not take it) and compensate wage levels need to be put in place. Moreover, stereotypes must be broken down, which is not necessarily something that one can legislate for.

Achieving greater gender equality requires not only a liberation for women but also for men. The stereotypes of the male breadwinner should be a thing of the past but there is still a residual notion of this. This also has implications for earnings (with women concentrated in low-paid sectors) and the role of men and women in the home. The statistics show that very few men take any responsibility for domestic tasks. A culture change is needed; it has started but the pace is too slow in many parts of Europe.

It might seem simplistic to reduce the policy mix to these three elements but an overhaul of the current system, especially a revolution in childcare, is what is needed. There is an over-reliance in some parts of Europe on part-time work. I believe that promoting part-time work, instead of concentrating our efforts on childcare, is not the right progressive approach to gender equality.

The proponents of part-time work argue that women want to work part-time. I concede that it might be the case that some mothers, just as some fathers, might want to work part-time during the early years of their children's lives. However, we cannot quote the figure of those working part-time as an indication of those who 'choose' to work part-time, because a lot of working parents simply do not have that choice due to under-investment in childcare and pre-schooling. We should not be satisfied with this second best alternative.

Moreover, part-time work is generally paid at a low level and at low seniority levels. In some member states it contributes significantly to the gender pay gap. For example, in the UK the gender pay gap in part-time work stands at over 40 per cent. This has implications for well-qualified women whose skills are underused when they work part-time.

Some have suggested that we need to focus on creating better quality part-time work. It might be the case that we can successfully encourage job-sharing of high-level posts in public services and charities. However, companies do not have the economic incentive to offer job shares, especially in systems in which it is more expensive to pay two people instead of one. Social democrats, however, are not necessarily in agreement on this. As I mentioned above the jury is still out on the progressive case for gender equality.

In conclusion, the demographic challenges we face add a fresh economic impetus for greater gender equality. European politicians and policy makers are beginning to realise that the only way to succeed in a globalised world with an ageing population is to enable women to both work more and have more children. The childcare revolution should be our top priority. There is also a strong economic case for this in terms of job creation. Enabling both parents to work full-time whilst balancing work and family commitments should be our aspiration, not some kind of halfway house in which a high percentage of women work part-time and are thus undervalued and underpaid.

References

Andersson, Magdalena (2005): Why gender equality?, in: Giddens, Anthony, Patrick Diamond (eds): The New Egalitarianism, Cambridge.

European Commission (2006): Report on Gender Equality, Brussels.

Esping-Andersen, Gøsta (2003): Women in the new welfare equilibrium, in: Auer, Peter, Bernanrd Gazier (eds): Future of Work, Employment And Social Protection: The Dynamics Of Change And The Protection Of Workers, Geneva.

Women in Social Democratic Politics

By Wendy Stokes

Social democracy benefits women. Around the world women earn less than men, they own less than men, they are less literate, less educated, there are fewer women than men in professional occupations and high status positions, and women are more subject to physical and sexual violence in and around the home than men. Social democracy equalises. Where social democratic policies are pursued, there is greater equality and this improves the lives of women as a group on all these measures and more, as has been clearly demonstrated in the work of Richard Wilkinson and others. The social democratic welfare state has been described as an instrument for the redistribution of wealth from men to women.

Since this is the case, you would think that women would unequivocally support social democratic politics both with their votes and with political activism. Women do vote for parties of the Left, but not in proportions radically different from those of their male counterparts. Gender gaps are interesting and variable, and politicians need to take account of them, but they do not show the vast differences that one might expect if women were, as a group, voting in their class interest. Women do join social democratic political parties and do run for office, but their party membership is not very different from that of men, and we see across Europe that women run for office and are elected in smaller proportions than men in parties of all persuasions. Despite such high profile figures as Angela Merkel and Margaret Thatcher, parties of the Left are, for the most part, more hospitable to women than those of the Right, but the picture is complicated and little can be taken for granted.

Here is the question: if social democracy is objectively more beneficial for women than most of the alternatives, how can its proponents persuade women voters of this? Parties have approached this from two directions: policies and people. The first is a traditional strategy: shape policies to serve the interests of the groups whose votes you seek to attract. The second is newer and more controversial: put up candidates who are members of the group whose votes you seek.

Parties fall into three different groups around the issues of getting more women elected. There are those that take the issue on and put pro-active measures in place; there are those that recognise a problem and exhort their members and officials to get busy, but avoid taking direct action; and there are those that do not consider the relative absence of women from elected office a problem. In general, parties of the Left make up the first and second groups, while parties of the Right make up the third, although the soft-right, like the Conservative Party in the United Kingdom (UK), is wising up, and far-right parties will deploy women as candidates and representatives strategically.

For political feminists and politically ambitious women the arguments are clear, but how does it look from the other side? Are there clear benefits to social democratic parties from the active promotion of women as candidates and elected officials? The following discussion will consider first the numbers and proportions of women in parliaments and parties around

Europe. It will then rehearse the arguments favouring more equal representation of women and men and the strategies and mechanisms that have been mobilised in order to achieve this. Finally, it will consider what we hope to achieve by improving the gender balance of elected representatives and whether this serves specifically social democratic goals.

Women in Parties and Parliaments in Europe

The proportion of women in the parliaments of Organization for Security and Co-operation in Europe (OSCE) member countries is 18.5 per cent (19.0 per cent in a single or lower house; 16.3 per cent in an upper house). However, this diminishes to 16.8 per cent (17.0 per cent in a single or lower house; 16.3 per cent in an upper house) when the Nordic countries are excluded – not surprisingly, since Nordic countries occupy four of the five top spots on the Inter-Parliamentary Union's international table of women's participation. Looking at the countries of the European Union, the proportion of women elected ranges from 45.3 per cent in Sweden to 9.1 per cent in Hungary.

The various countries of the European Union (EU) tend to elect more women to the European Parliament than they do to their own parliaments. Thus, 57.9 per cent of Sweden's MEPs are women, as are 37.5 per cent of those returned from Hungary – although there are exceptions: Finland, for example, returned a slightly smaller proportion of female MEPs in 2004 than members of its own parliament in 2003. The lowest proportion of female MEPs is to be found among the Poles, only 13 per cent, while Cyprus and Malta did not elect any women to the European Parliament in 2004.

Parties of the Left across Europe tend to return a greater proportion of female representatives to national and local assemblies than do parties of the Right. In France, where female representation has always been low (prior to the implementation of parity, see below) the highest numbers of women deputies were usually from the Left: in 1986 female deputies made up 9.9 per cent of the socialist group elected, whereas the Right had only

3 per cent. The 2002 election, (post parity) returned 16.3 and 19 per cent female representatives from the two main left-wing parties, while the two main right-wing parties returned 10.4 and 6.8 per cent. In Spain the Socialist Party (PSOE) has consistently returned a higher percentage of women than other parties, as has the Labour Party in the UK. The same pattern appears to hold in the former communist countries, for example in Hungary, where politics is male-dominated and masculine in political culture, the left-wing party, MSzP, returned 12.9 per cent, the highest proportion of female MPs, at the 2002 election.

Similarly, when we look at the political groups in the European Parliament there is considerable variation in the proportion of women members in each, although women figure far more strongly in the groups to the Left of the political spectrum than in those to the Right. In the Green/European Free Alliance Group 47.6 per cent of the members are women, the Group of the Alliance of Liberals and Democrats for Europe has 41 per cent, and the Parliamentary Group of European Socialists has 38 per cent. By contrast, in the Group of the European People's Party (Christian Democrats) and European Democrats 23 per cent of members are women, the Union for the Europe of Nations Group has 16.8 per cent and the Independence/Democracy Group has 9 per cent. An exception appears to be the Confederation Group of European United Left/Nordic Green Left with 29 per cent women.

The Arguments for More Equal Representation
Does any of this matter except as a rather minority and obsessive pursuit within political science? Arguments in favour of actively promoting the election of women fall into three categories: equal opportunities, best value, and effective democracy. The first of these is the easiest to deal with and support. The goal of facilitating equal opportunities is by now deeply embedded in EU policy, and it is widely accepted that simply having anti-discrimination legislation and regulation is not enough. In addition to the existence of non-discriminatory rules and regulations, prac-

tices and outcomes have to be demonstrably non-discriminatory. Accordingly, despite the absence of laws prohibiting the election of women, if we see that very few women are elected we will, at the very least, suspect that discrimination of some sort may have taken place along the way. We shall therefore be obliged to find ways to achieve more equality of opportunity.

Equality of opportunity relates to the second argument given above: best value. With elected representatives, as with any other important occupation, we want to make sure that the most able people are in post; this might be termed getting the best value from them. If our representatives are not drawn from the widest possible constituency – if groups of people do not take part in the selection process – we may suspect that we are not getting the best possible representatives and representation.

The third argument is the most contentious: effective democracy. This suggests that our representative body should include people from across the range of differences in the community. Further, it argues that if it does not, if representatives are drawn from a narrow section of the community and the parliament does not include people from significant groups, the representative legitimacy of the parliament is undermined. With regard to women, this argument has been developed along the lines of a politics of presence by Anne Phillips and others adopting her model. This contends that women's presence among elected representatives is important because women as women have different experiences and perspectives from men. These experiences and perspectives, which men are less likely to have access to, are important for political policy and decision-making.

Thus, the project to increase the number of women elected can be pursued from two quite different perspectives. Stripping political systems of all forms of discrimination and opening them up to politically ambitious and able women is an equal opportunities programme that does not necessarily have any other ideological content; when opening the political agenda to women's experiences and perspectives is added, this is a feminist programme.

191

Equality Strategies and Mechanisms

It is usually argued that while cultural and socio-economic explanations of women's relative absence from elected office (and of differences between countries) are intuitively appealing, political variables are in fact the most significant. There is some correlation between religion, the date at which women got the vote, the presence of women in professional occupations and the proportion of women in a parliament (Mercedes Mateo Diaz summarises the research on this). However, the strongest correlation is with the electoral system. Generally, proportional representation and multi-member constituency systems return more women than do first-past-the-post and single member constituency systems. In addition, many (but not all) of the countries with high proportions of elected women operate some sort of quota system.

Some 75 countries internationally operate, or have operated, electoral quotas for women; in twelve of these the quota is of parliamentary seats that are set aside for women; in a further 25 there is a statutory quota. Among countries of the European Union only France and Belgium use a statutory quota while parties in a number of EU countries have voluntarily used quotas. These include parties in Finland, Germany, the Netherlands, Austria, Spain, Portugal, Italy, the UK and Luxemburg. According to Norris,

> By 2000, among 76 relevant European parties (with at least ten members in the lower house), almost half (35 parties) use gender quotas, and two dozen of these have achieved levels of female representation in the lower house of parliament over 24%. Among the European parties using gender quotas, on average one third (33%) of their elected representatives were women. By contrast, in European parties without gender quotas, only 18% of their members of parliament were women. (Norris 2004)

Quotas may be mandatory or voluntary and may be used at party or parliamentary level. They are more easily introduced in a PR system, where manipulating positions on a party list can be used. In EU countries quotas are mostly at party level, and more often voluntary than mandatory. Broadly left-wing parties are more likely to use quota systems than conservative parties, and tend to include more women as representatives even without having a quota. In Europe, parties of the Left started to introduce quotas in the 1980s. These included green, social democrat, communist, socialist and labour parties.

Quotas are often associated with the Nordic countries, but this is to make the mistake of generalising from the example of Norway, which is probably the paradigm of quota use: only one party in Sweden has a quota and Danish parties ceased to use them in 1996. The relatively high numbers of women elected in all the Nordic countries appears to be due to political culture and activism as much as quotas, for example, the Swedish principle of *Varannan Damernas*, 'Every Other Seat a Women's Seat', which has been in operation since the 1980s.

In the UK, the Labour party has managed to circumvent the apparent conservatism of the first-past-the-post, single member constituency system by using women-only shortlists in a proportion of key constituencies, in addition to making use of the additional-member provision in elections to the new regional assemblies. Enabling legislation was passed in 2002. In 1999 France took the unique step of legislating for sex-parity in party candidacies; this has proved problematic so far with parties apparently struggling to find enough candidates, and some parties preferring to pay the penalty for not meeting the parity requirement. Nonetheless, the percentage of women elected has increased.

In a few countries women's parties have been created to counter exclusion. These tend to appear where the promises of equality have not been met and/or where there are traditions of separate women's organisations. The Women's Coalition of Northern Ireland seems to be a response to the resolute exclusion of women and women's issues from a political system that prioritises equality between religious groups. Women's parties in former Soviet republics and other formerly communist countries seem to be both a response to exclusion and the continuation of a tradition of separate women's organisations. The creation of a women's party in Greece is a rather different affair, since this appears to be a party promoting the support of women's traditional social roles.

Will Improving the Gender Balance Make Parties More Appealing?

Improving the balance of men and women in elected office has become a goal of both women's organisations and political parties. While women's organisations are driven by a range of motivations, including the political ambitions of members, social justice, democracy and feminist principles, it is probably fair to say that political parties are most strongly driven by the urge to win votes. Of course, individual party members, activists and representatives may want to get more women into office for any number of reasons, but a party as an institution is focused on gaining power via votes.

Political parties, initially of the Left but increasingly from across the political spectrum, are paying attention to women's votes. When women were first included in the franchise there was considerable concern about what they would do with their votes. The parties of the Left that supported the vote for women from the perspective of democratic justice were worried that women would use their votes in support of conservative parties. Parties of the Right that did not in general support women's enfranchisement rather expected to benefit from it. In the event it turned out that women placed their votes in much the same way as men of the same demographic, although the belief that women are more conservative than men has persisted.

The thesis that women are more conservative than men when it comes to voting has been carefully unpicked by political scientists over recent years. The picture that has emerged is complex and illuminating about the voting behaviour of both men and women. By and large, men and women of the same demographic vote similarly. However, differences do appear that are quite specific to, on the one hand, time and place, and, on the other, to the age and socio-economic position of voters. What was referred to as a 'gender gap' when it became apparent that women in the USA were voting for the Democratic Party in larger proportions than men, is in fact a very complex phenomenon. From her extensive data analysis Pippa Norris claimed in 1996 that there was, 'considerable variation cross-nationally in the gender gap, with women more right-wing than men in Britain, Australia, Luxemburg and Italy, while women are more left-wing in Germany, Spain, Portugal, and the USA'. She concluded, 'The results suggest that the conventional wisdom about women's greater conservatism across Europe is no longer valid' (Norris 1996). By 2003 Inglehart and Norris were finding further consolidation of this trend in western Europe and concluded that women held more 'left-leaning' values that men in most countries (Inglehart and Norris 2003).

So, research suggests that the voting behaviour of men and women will be similarly shaped by events and policies much of the time, but may be affected differently on occasion. For example, De Vaus and McAllister found that women were more opposed to war, the use of force, nuclear energy, and nuclear weapons than men, and were more likely to support welfare programmes and environmentalism, and Inglehart and Norris refer to differences in 'value orientations' particularly with regard to 'post-materialism, the role of government, and gender equality'. Whatever may have happened in the past, conservative parties today cannot rely on any difference being to their advantage among female voters any more than parties of the Left can rely on having the edge with men: at one point in the UK young men were more likely to vote conservatively than young women.

There is a growing assumption that having more women as candidates and elected representatives makes a party more appealing to women – and possibly to some men. This assumption exists in an uneasy balance with worries about whether people are prepared to vote for a woman. Women's preference for voting for women is a frequently repeated credo. Repeated at least as often is the claim that, contrary to the belief that women favour voting for women, they in fact are resistant to voting for women. Neither contention appears to have much basis in empirical research; however, some findings from the USA in 1997 suggested that female voters might prefer female candidates. There is a further suggestion that American women not only vote Democrat in slightly higher numbers than men, they do so in greater numbers when the candidate is a woman – and in some recorded instances the vote reversed when the Republican candidate was a woman.

Similar results emerged from research into the 2001 general election in the UK.

> The presence of women as representatives increases women's activism. In seats where a woman MP was elected in 2001 women's turnout was 4% higher than men's. Women were also less interested in the election campaign and less likely to say that they would volunteer to work for a candidate or party in seats with a male MP. Women were far more likely to agree that 'government benefits people like me' in constituencies with a female MP (49% compared to 38%). Where a man represented the seat, this gap reversed. (Electoral Commission 2004)

Nonetheless, getting good data on voting disaggregated by sex is a tricky task – for the very good reason that it is close to impossible to separate out the results of a secret ballot! Asking people how they would prefer to vote is unreliable, although exit polls can include the sex of the voter. What we do know, thanks to recent research, is that people as a whole are not much bothered by the sex of a candidate, and that in certain circumstances female candidates benefit.

There is some research that shows bias against women candidates to be a factor in voting preference – for example that undertaken by Fox and Smith who compared college students in Wyoming and California. It is not accidental that much of the research cited so far is from the USA. In American politics individual candidates have a far higher profile than they do in Europe, where party dominates candidacy and policy at elections, so in the US individual characteristics, including sex, loom larger than they do elsewhere.

The introduction of women-only shortlists by the Labour Party in the UK in 1997 offered an opportunity for looking at voter responses to female candidates. From their research into this election Studlar and McAllister conclude that: 'voters did not discriminate to any extent between men and women candidates', further, 'within the Labour party, candidates from women-only shortlists did substantially better in attracting votes than their male counterparts'.

Would Improving the Gender
Balance Benefit Social Democracy?

Beyond the claim that the election of women in more or less equal numbers with men is democratically desirable is the suggestion that women's equal participation in politics will generate policies that benefit women. A further suggestion is that

> a critical mass of women in political institutions would also initiate change in broader policies of development and international relations – for example, by developing policies of peace and non-violent conflict resolution, access to and protection of the full body of human rights, sustainable and socially just development and placing people above profits and [...] would transform the very nature of power and the practice of politics through the values of cooperation and collaboration [...] that women would play politics differently and practise power accountably. (Batliwala 2005)

This is the most difficult argument of the many around women's political participation both to defend in the abstract and to demonstrate from research. As an abstract argument it runs the risk of descending into sex essentialism and claims that women are essentially something while men are essentially something else, rather than making the less controversial claim that as outsiders with different sorts of experiences from the insiders, women might bring different insights and habits to the political arena – if given a chance to do so. The values described above are clearly social democratic, even if social democratic parties have rather lost sight of them.

Research by the Inter-Parliamentary Union found that 89 per cent of the female representatives surveyed, from sixty-five countries, believed that they had a special responsibility to represent women's needs and interests. Research in the UK, the Nordic countries and the USA found similar responses from elected women. Looking at what people do, rather than what they say they want to do, there is some evidence that women in office do support such policies a little more than their male equivalents, and that increased numbers of elected women leads to the adoption of policies more beneficial to women. Barbara Burrell's research in the US Congress, Manon Tremblay's in the Canadian Parliament and the work of Marian Sawer on the Australian Senate all found that female representatives were more likely to raise issues of particular relevance to women than men were.

There is also some research that suggests that elected women are slightly more inclined to support more general liberal issues than their male counterparts. For example, looking at the US Congress, Barbara Burrell found that as early as the 1960s more female representatives in the USA supported the Civil Rights Act and the Equal Rights Amendment than their male counterparts. Moreover, in terms of voting patterns, she found that Democrat women were the most liberal group and Republican men the least.

Conclusion

To conclude, social democracy objectively benefits women as a group by countering gendered differences in interests. These include gendered differences in wages, opportunities and family life as well as concerns about the environment and military conflict. Social democratic politics does this through egalitarian, environmental and welfare legislation and provision. Women respond to this by voting for social democratic parties in slightly higher proportions than men. There is a growing interest in enhancing that tendency by making parties' appearances more women-friendly via the inclusion of more elected women alongside men who espouse feminist policies. Some research and a lot of rather unsubstantiated (but appealing) rhetoric on the part of both politicians and prominent women support this. A further consideration derives from the assertion that women in office will encourage the creation of women-friendly policies and a way of doing politics that is more appealing to women. Again, there is some research that supports this, but not much since the presence of women is a new and still growing phenomenon and therefore hard to test. If this is the case then a virtuous circle is formed: the election of more women leads to better policies that attract more women voters. It is a tenuous contention at present, but it would seem that there is nothing to be lost from getting more women elected and there may be much to be gained.

References

Batliwala, Srilatha (2005): Women Transforming Power?, www.opendemocracy.net, 6th October.

Bergqvist, Christina et al (1999): Equal Democracies? Gender and Politics in the Nordic Countries, Oslo.

Bird, Karen (2003): Who are the Women? Where are the Women? And What Difference Can they Make? Effects of Gender Parity in French Municipal Elections, in: *French Politics*, vol. 3, no. 1.

Burrell, Barbara (1994): A Woman's Place in the House, Ann Arbor.

Childs, Sarah (2004): New Labour's Women MPs: Women Representing Women, Oxford.

De Vaus, D., I. McAllister (1989): The Changing Politics of Women: Gender and Political Alignment in 11 Nations, in: *European Journal of Political Research*, vol. 25, 241-262.

Electoral Commission (2004): Gender and Political Participation, London.

Ford, L. E. (2002): Women and Politics: the Pursuit of Equality, Boston.

Fox, Richard L., Eric A. N. Smith (1998): The Role of Candidate Sex in Voter Decision-Making, in: *Political Psychology*, vol. 19, no. 2.

Galligan, Yvonne, Manon Tremblay (eds) (2005): Sharing Power: Women, Parliament, Democracy, Aldershot.

Inglehart, Ronald, Pippa Norris (2003): Rising Tide: Gender Equality and Cultural Change Around the World, Cambridge.

Mateo Diaz, Mercedes (2005): Representing Women: Female Legislators in West European Parliaments, Colchester.

Norris, Pippa (1996): Mobilising the Women's Vote: The Gender-Generation Gap in Voting Behaviour, in: *Parliamentary Affairs*, vol. 49, no. 2.

Norris, Pippa (2004): Building Political Parties, Cambridge.

Phillips, Anne (1995): The Politics of Presence, Oxford.

Selzer R. A., J. Newman, M. V. Leighton (1997): Sex as a
Political Variable, Boulder.
Sineau, Mariette (2005): France, in: Yvonne Galligan,
Manon Tremblay (eds): Sharing Power. Women, Parliament,
Democracy, Aldershot.

Studlar, D. T., I. McAllister (1998): Candidate Gender and
Voting in the 1997 British General Election. Did Labour Quotas
Matter?, in: *Journal of Legislative Studies*, vol. 4, no. 3.

Tremblay, Manon (2003): Women's Representational Role
in Australia and Canada. The Impact of Political Context, in:
Australian Journal of Political Science, vol. 38, no. 2.

Wilkinson, Richard G. (2005): The Impact of Inequality,
London.

The Freedom We Mean

By Hubertus Heil

Freedom is a grand concept and there is much talk of it in Germany at present. For social democrats, freedom – flanked by justice and solidarity – is the supreme basic value. The fact that freedom is currently on the lips of politicians of all hues should put us on our toes. Even the German Federal Chancellor made it the key issue in her government policy statement.

For many people of my generation – particularly those who were born and brought up in the old Federal Republic – 'freedom' was taken for granted. Over time it degenerated into a hackneyed concept and was left to the advertising industry to exploit at will. 'Freedom' thus became a brand attribute for credit cards and cheap flights.

In the meantime our society has begun a new quest for meaning and fundamental values; the time has come to retrieve the concept of freedom from the world of marketing and put it back into the political debate. The formation of a grand coalition will not hinder this new quest. On the contrary, it is likely to expedite it. In essence, any debate on the concept of 'freedom' revolves around the classical distinction made by the philosopher Isaiah Berlin between negative freedom (the freedom from something) and positive freedom (the freedom to do something).

In line with the teachings of Friedrich August von Hayek, economic liberals are quite content with negative freedom. Guido Westerwelle talks a great deal about freedom – as chairman of the Free Democratic Party, that is part of his job description. In his reply to the Chancellor he equated tax increases with a lack of freedom. For him freedom means radical denationalisation and the release of the *homo economicus* from all social commitments. Freedom is thus reduced to freedom of economic pursuit.

By contrast, Udo Di Fabio, a conservative judge at the Constitutional Court, stresses in his much-acclaimed book *Die Kultur der Freiheit* (The Culture of Freedom) that freedom is inconceivable without social ties and obligations. The position he adopts is thus antithetical to socially irresponsible ultra-liberalism. So far, so good. At the same time, however, he considers that free individuals should do something and give something before they start asking society for something. That sounds good too, but while Di Fabio's point may be significant it ignores the social and very practical prerequisites for freedom.

The realisation that individual freedom is crucially important but that it depends on certain social and political conditions is one of the fundamental tenets of social democracy. In his farewell speech as SPD chairman Willy Brandt remarked: 'If I had to state what, apart from peace, is more important to me than anything else I would say without any ifs or buts: freedom. Freedom for many, not for the few. Freedom of conscience and speech. Freedom from need and fear, too'. For him freedom was by no means controlled happiness but the release of the creative skills invested in man.

It is not least the political Left that has achieved a good deal in releasing those creative skills. That everybody can find their place in society through their own efforts and that everybody has the theoretical opportunity to live their life according to their own designs is a very recent development in the history of mankind. It presumes equal freedoms for women and men and the chance to overcome social barriers. One of the main concerns driving social democrats has always been to give people opportunities and not to pigeonhole them for the rest of their lives on account of their social origins.

How free is our society then? A young person living on income support in the second generation and growing up in a residential ghetto somewhere in the suburbs without acquiring any school-leaving qualifications or finding a trainee position can do as he pleases within the bounds of the law. But is such a person free? In theory, nobody will stop him learning new things and standing on his own two feet. But in real life – which is what politics should be about – this young person has virtually no chance if he is not systematically pushed and encouraged. Or to take a different example: a businessman is not free to fire his employees as he thinks fit. Laws and contracts prevent him from doing so and thus limit his negative freedom. Would society be freer if he could hire and fire at will?

It is no accident that freedom is given pride of place in the code of basic social democratic values. It includes negative freedom, in other words the freedom from fear, need, paternalism, bureaucracy and discrimination. But it also includes positive freedom, in other words the freedom to seize the opportunities life offers and act on one's own responsibility.

Social democrats do not place blind faith in the state. For us, as for others, restrictive and unnecessary red tape and excessive calls for statistics and reports do not rank amongst our political objectives. We know that, for the sake of the country's future, we need both a dynamic economy, a civic society based on the principle of solidarity and a state that is capable of taking the requisite action. The latter serves not merely to provide the economy and society with public goods that the market alone cannot supply. In a democracy, a functioning state is essential to ensure that the strength of the law prevails and not the law of the strong.

We social democrats want people to be emancipated and capable of mature judgement. Free people are informed; they face up to reality, represent their interests and act in a responsible manner on their own behalf and that of others. This emancipatory potential that is inherent in freedom does not develop of its own accord. Enabling it to blossom is an active and conscious social achievement. Those who talk of freedom today should not forget to mention responsibility. Human rights and human duties apply here in a comprehensive sense. Those who derive advantage from their income or wealth have a duty to make an appropriate contribution to the well-being of all.

This is what distinguishes our concept of freedom from that of the economic liberals, who see positive freedom as posing a threat to negative freedom and thus cannot redeem the promise of freedom for a large number of people. A policy of freedom presumes the capacity to exercise freedom. It must place its faith in equal opportunities for the future, guarantee social rights and reinforce social standards and values. This stems from the realisation that one's own freedom is always that of others, too.

Putin's Russia: Love and Hatred Towards the EU

By Silvio Pons

Although an essential strategic resource, the enlargement of the European Union is now reaching its limit, presenting with increasing clarity and inevitability both its inclusive and an exclusive aspect: it no longer aims solely at shifting the European Union's (EU) space, but at establishing a boundary. At present, we can see that to the east, this boundary has been extended to include the space of the former Soviet Union in addition to the Baltic states, and all the way to Ukraine, excluding Russia. As far as the EU's architecture is concerned, this is fully understandable. But Russia then becomes an essential test for the EU's future foreign policy – much more than the 'politics of proximity' would appear to predict.

At present, Russia is not an international political priority for any of the leading global players, nor does it truly play this role, despite trying to claim it. It is a country largely dependent on Western financial, commercial and technological resources for its economic rebirth, and partnership with the EU plays a leading role from this standpoint. Its ruling class – and still more, its public opinion – continues to claim a European identity, without renouncing a statist and geopolitical dimension distinct from the EU. Moscow no longer presents a threat to Europe, and Western intervention in the former Yugoslavia casts light on Russia's weak reaction to a crisis that directly affected its long-standing traditions in international affairs. In central eastern Europe the limits of Moscow's influence – harshly underlined by recent events in Ukraine – are clear enough to warrant no further comment. In brief, Russia is much less important to Europe than Europe is to Russia. After all, the reality that we are getting used to – a reality taken for granted from our standpoint, but unheard of for those with memories of the last century – is one of an inward-looking Russia presenting no challenge at all. All this has allowed us to understate the importance of its distancing from Europe, which appears to be the result of the EU's expansion process.

The European agenda was effectively influenced by Poland and the Baltic states as a result of their determination to establish the EU's eastern boundary in the most exclusive terms. This is an approach that takes Russia's civil and political incongruity for granted, and thus does not concern itself with feeding the former superpower, fostering the growing divergence between the legiti-mate Europeanist aspirations of the former Soviet countries on the one hand and the post-imperial frustrations of the Russian Federation on the other. But here a paradox is created. The promise of democracy and well-being accompanying European expansion does not only not involve Russia – it is being made while Russia is taking a different road – but may even be seen as a factor contributing to what is perceived as Russian involution. There is room for doubt as to whether or not this is in the EU's true interest. There is a great difference between bordering on a Russia sufficiently prosperous and cooperative, more reliable as a constitutional state and unleashed from its imperial heritage, or on a Russia oscillating between instrumentalised partnerships, a sense of exclusion and post-imperial nationalism.

The summit between Bush and Putin held in Bratislava in February 2005 provided a glimpse of America's changing attitude towards the democratic quality of its Russian partner, appearing to herald a foreign policy motif for the American President's second administration and an additional challenge for the EU. It remains to be seen whether the EU will be able to meet this challenge. For the time being, it may easily be seen that neither Putin's meetings with Chirac and Schröder in March nor the summit between the EU and Russia in May 2005 produced a high-profile strategy. Thus, the main change commanding our attention is rather Putin's attitude. In Bratislava, and even more recently, he has presented commitment to democracy as an irreversible choice linked to his country's vital interests. He has not raised the traditional argument of non-interference in internal affairs. Instead, Putin has insisted that democracy must be adapted to various national situations, alluding to Russia's inclination to a privileged order and state prestige over any manifestation of disintegration and disorder. He thus invoked the legitimacy of his own centralising action, which is at the same time a clear rejection of any universalist democratic thrust. It is likely that this response by Putin bears out those who maintain that public pressure, like that adopted by Bush, can achieve the opposite effect. But the point is that Putin's words mark a limit to Russia's strategic partnership with the West, as apparently inaugurated after 9/11. Now, not only the foreign policy adopted by Putin in the post-Soviet area and the Middle East but also his claim of legitimacy for an authoritarian democracy show the prevalently strategic nature of Russian policy towards the West.

Consequently, Russia proposes a thrust towards multipolarism as based upon political and cultural diversity and upon power politics – potentially incompatible with the multilateralist perspective that is the very heart of EU's international role. The relative activism of Russian policy towards China and India (and more recently even towards Turkey) must be seen as the search for converging thrusts rather than strategic alliances. The development of international politics after 9/11 has made an essential contribution to this development in Putin's policy. On the one hand, the militarising trend of the 'war on terrorism' in Iraq has boosted Putin's desire to internationalise the war in Chechnya, legitimising Russia's military methods. From this standpoint, the alliance with Chirac and Schröder had no stable political significance other than reinforcing a multipolar vision implicitly more radical than the neo-Gaullist position. On the other hand, the wave of democracy in the countries of the former Soviet Union took place precisely while Russia was limiting the range of its political reforms, also as a consequence of the Chechen scourge and its resulting terrorism. These two elements show a significant convergence that fits into a longer-term process.

Currently, two essential aspects of Russia's transition are nearing achievement. The first is the birth of a strong power, which has put an end to the weakness of the institution of the presidency since the time of its establishment – and has directed all its energies towards keeping the Federation from falling apart. The second is the sterilisation of what little political pluralism and parliamentary democracy existed after the collapse of the USSR. In truth, the consolidation of the presidency is not merely the affirmation of personal power, but reflects a restoration of the state's authority after a period of perilous disintegration. But the point is that Putin appears to offer a solution different from that of his predecessors: abandoning the attempt to yoke the introduction of the market to a radical reform of the political system, and, instead, restoring the state's authority.

In this sense, the rise of Putin put an end to a phase in Russian history that had been opened by Gorbachev, while the recurring comparisons in the Russian press between the figure of the President and that of Andropov are less superficial than one may think – they do not merely refer to the common link of the KGB. Market authoritarianism and the affirmed continuity of the state (which does not even refrain from re-evaluating Stalin in a nationalist/patriotic vein) are presented as ingredients of Russia's international integration achieved without Westernisation. This is the ambiguous basis on which Putin has reconstituted an international role for the country, putting an end to the Yeltsin era's oscillation between cooperation and competition with the West. Today, the idea of integration between Russia and Europe promoted by Putin goes no further than a highly selective and conditional involvement.

Russia's ambivalence in its relationship with Europe is a cliché of historical and political discourse. The liberal philosopher Isaiah Berlin, deeply steeped in Russian culture, spoke of Russia's 'peculiar amalgam of love and hatred' towards Europe, but firmly believed in its essentially westward-leaning character. On the other hand, Russian historian Mikhail Gefter believed that Russia's place 'in the orbit' of European expansion could not change a deeper truth: Russia was historically 'the threshold and the limit' of this expansion. These views appear to translate quite clearly into the contradictory reality of our time; and yet they remain unresolved. Putin's 'controlled democracy' may be considered a Russian internal issue to be criticised, but one essentially without implications for Europe or even seen in a positive light as a source of the country's stability. In turn, Russia's multipolar thrust may be deemed too weak to truly influence the international system, or, alternatively, as a useful buffer of anti-Americanism. But taken together, these two factors outline a perspective that brings us face to face with all the problems inherent in the main challenge of our times: the difficult relationship between security and the expansion of democracy.